UNDERSTANDING THE SPIRITUALITY OF TRUE STEWARDSHIP

God's Love in Action

Christopher N. Sealey

AdventSource
www.adventsource.org
800.328.0525

Table of Contents

Preface

This book represents an important milestone in my life. God has given me the opportunity to share His truth about stewardship with many audiences. All along the way I have been motivated to take His principles of stewardship to a wider audience, therefore this book is a step towards that goal.

This work contains many passages of Scripture, as well as quotations from other Christian writers, interwoven with explanations and comments to aid the reader in understanding the spirituality of stewardship.

I am particularly grateful to my wife Deborah, my children Joshua and Rosalie and my parents for their support and encouragement throughout the years. I wish to express my deep and lasting appreciation to the members of the Breath of Life Seventh-day Adventist Church, Rochester, NY and to my friend and previous Pastor, Roger R. Wade, for their support and feedback in refining and simplifying some of the more complex spiritual concepts of stewardship.

Finally, I would like to express my gratitude to Dr. Bertram Melbourne and Pastor Victoria D. Harrison for their input and advice on the manuscript.

> *Let each one [give] as he has made up his own mind*
> *and purposed in his heart, not reluctantly or sorrow-*
> *fully or under compulsion, for God loves (He takes*

pleasure in, prizes above other things, and is unwilling to abandon or to do without) a cheerful (joyous) giver [whose heart is in his giving].

2 Corinthians 9:7 (AMP)

Introduction

Albert Einstein once said: "During the last century, and part of the one before, it was widely held that there was an [irreconcilable] conflict between knowledge and belief. The opinion prevailed among advanced minds that it was time that belief should be replaced increasingly by knowledge; belief that did not itself rest on knowledge was superstition, and as such had to be opposed." [1]

There are so many people in the world today who believe in principles of which they have no knowledge of their origin or accuracy. These beliefs are passed on from person to person and from generation to generation. These beliefs become transformed into actions that have no real meaning or substance; these actions constitute mere rituals.

Unfortunately, stewardship happens to be one of those things that many people believe in and practice, but very few of them have a clear knowledge or understanding of what it really means or its significance in God's plan for mankind. They practice stewardship as a mere ritual.

Hundreds of books and articles have been written on this subject but they all assume that the audience has a fundamental knowledge of stewardship.

Numerous seminars and workshops have been conducted on this subject, yet all of the material presented starts with the premise that everyone knows the fundamental reason why God implemented the system of stewardship. Most of the focus seems to be on the promised benefits obtained from adherence to the principles of stewardship and on the development of sophisticated techniques to develop a lifestyle that conforms to that of a faithful steward.

For a while I, too, read the books and attended the workshops and began to practice the principles that would make me a faithful steward — a manager of God's property. But I yearned for a deeper understanding of the true meaning of stewardship. I got tired of hearing the same rhetoric from the pulpit or seeing ten (10) minute skits performed to act out how a faithful steward should respond to appeals for church projects.

I did not want to adopt the incorrect paradigm of stewardship as a tool for Christians to manage their money and material possessions; nor did I want to think like a financial investor, that if I give to God then He will open the windows of heaven and give me more than I invested.

God never implements a system or a process without taking the time to explain His reason(s) for doing so. In 1 Corinthians 2:12-15, the Bible states that the Holy Spirit teaches us the meaning of God's word and He helps us to accept its wisdom. Under the direction and guidance of the Holy Spirit, we begin to comprehend God's principles of true stewardship and to enact them in our lives.

When we desire to understand God's principles, we must search the entire Bible for His truth. We can't search the Old Testament in isolation or work from the New Testament alone. We must go back to Genesis where it all began and prayerfully work our way to Revelation. Every principle of God began in the Garden of Eden, points to the Cross of Calvary and ends in Revelation with the second coming of Christ. The Holy Spirit inspired men to write the Bible (2 Timothy 3:16) and it is He alone who will inspire men to interpret it; Holy Spirit in equals Holy Spirit out.

It would be unwise to consider only the Scripture verse(s) in the book of Malachi and attempt to fully understand or teach God's principles of stewardship. It is a good thing to read books that help you study the Bible, but ultimately the Bible interprets itself. The Bible is a living book; it doesn't have a shelf life. The original Greek word used in 2 Timothy 3:16 is ***theopneustos***[2] which means

"God breathed into". The first time we read "God breathed into" something (Genesis 2:7) that thing became alive and was known as man. Because God breathed into the Scripture, it became the living word of God capable of interpreting itself and changing the lives of its readers. Since God's word is a living word, then God's principles written in His word are everlasting. An analysis of the Levitical system of offerings, given to the Israelites around 1440 BC, will reveal His principles of stewardship for us today.

It is my prayer that the Holy Spirit will reveal to you from this book and the Bible, God's principles concerning the spirituality of true stewardship. He created us in His image and likeness and He knows that we are intelligent beings, so He placed in the Bible all His reasons for His actions.

Jesus said, *"Ask, and it will be given to you; seek, and you will find; knock, and it will be opened to you"*(Matthew 7:7). So together let us seek the answers from the Bible to the following questions:

- Why did God implement the system of stewardship?
- What is the true spiritual significance of stewardship?
- When and how did stewardship all begin?
- What is the meaning of all the symbolisms used in the Bible to represent offerings and sacrifices that were offered to God?
- 1 Corinthians 10: 26 reads: *"for the earth is the Lord's, and all its fullness.* Then why would God want anything from me?
- If everything I had comes from God, then why would He want some of it back? What does He plan to do with it? Is He going to give it to somebody else?
- Are the principles of stewardship upheld in the New Testament?
- In this modern day and age, should we really be practicing stewardship?
- Was tithing abolished in the New Testament?

The word steward is used fifteen (15) times in the Bible. It comes from the Greek word *oikonomos*[3], which means "the manager of a household" or "the manager of a specific area within the household". The work of the steward was called management or stewardship. Since the household and its goods did not belong to him but to the owner, the steward was responsible to the owner for the way he carried out his stewardship responsibilities. For example, in the parable of the unjust steward, the steward is asked to give an account of his stewardship (Luke 16:2).

God is the Owner and He has entrusted various gifts to us. We are His stewards, and we are also required to give an account to Him concerning the way we conduct our stewardship responsibilities. Everything that we own belongs to Him. *The earth is the Lord's, and all its fullness, the world and those who dwell therein* (Psalm 24:1). He requires us to exercise careful and faithful management of the things that He has entrusted to us.

> A mark of a careful and faithful manager is that he uses what has been entrusted to him in a way that is consistent with the wishes of the owner. Christian stewardship can thus be defined as the Christian's careful and faithful management of everything that God has entrusted to him. Another way of putting it: Stewardship is managing God's resources to carry out God's mission.[4]

Understanding the spirituality of stewardship establishes in our minds God's sovereignty, His ownership, and His love for us and requires us to respond appropriately in love.

The more I searched the Bible the more I discovered God's reasons for implementing stewardship. True stewardship is not a man-made concept to raise money. Stewardship was designed and implemented by God for man. When we follow God's principles of stewardship, we obtain a glimpse into the mind of God concerning His plan of salvation. Once an individual becomes convinced of God's principles and convicted by the Holy Spirit that individual would follow the ways of God.

The Bible says in John 12:32, *"And I, if I am lifted up from the earth, will draw all peoples to Myself"*. When God places in your mind His principles of true stewardship, the Holy Spirit transcends you from the mundane things of the world to the important and meaningful things in life. This allows you to realize fulfillment in your Christian experience.

This book does not focus on the mechanics of practicing stewardship, but on the spiritual significance of its principles. Therefore, this book contains no gimmicks, no clever plans for budgeting to accommodate giving; it contains no testimonials from individuals who have received bigger homes and boats because they have given huge sums of money to their favorite charity, church or non-profit organization.

As you read the pages of this book, it is my hope and prayer that what the Holy Spirit has revealed to me, He will reveal to you.

I invite you to read this book, so that your belief in the spirituality of true stewardship will rest on knowledge — knowledge gleamed from the word of God.

References:

1. Albert Einstein on Knowledge- *http://nico.rave.org/quo_2_ein_knowledge.htm*
2. Greek #2315 - *Strong's Dictionary of Hebrew and Greek Words*
3. Greek #3623 - *Strong's Dictionary of Hebrew and Greek Words*
4. *Christian Stewardship of Possessions – Compelled by the Love of Christ* by David J. Valleskey (August 1989)

"And walk in love, as Christ also
has loved us and given Himself for us,
an offering and a sacrifice to God for
a sweet-smelling aroma."

Ephesians 5:2

1

When and How Did Stewardship Begin?

In the Beginning...

To fully understand any biblical system or principle, one must first understand how and when it was established and to whom it applies. To understand the principles of true stewardship, as ordained by God, we must first revisit the Garden of Eden, since it represents the beginning of the human race.

In Genesis 1:27, 31 the Bible states,

So God created man in His own image; in the image of God He created him; male and female He created them. Then God saw everything that He had made, and indeed it was very good. So the evening and the morning were the sixth day.

There are seven references to the term good in Genesis Chapter 1 (vv. 4, 10, 12, 18, 21, 25, 31). The Hebrew word for good is ***tobe***[1] and it means "perfect", "beautiful" or "complete". Therefore when God created Adam and Eve, they were perfect, beautiful and complete in every aspect because they were created in His perfect image. There was no sin in their lives. God walked amongst Adam and Eve in the Garden of Eden and talked face to face with them. They actually saw the face of God and communicated directly with Him. There was no sin in their lives so they were close to God, and they enjoyed a sincere relationship with God their creator.

In their perfect form, Adam and Eve enjoyed a holy communion with God and He with them. As long as they remained sinless, they continued to be close to God and they were able to communicate directly with Him in a very personal and direct manner. Prior to sin entering the world, the relationship between Adam and Eve and that between them and God was the way that He intended it to be. We were created by God to worship Him and to exist in His presence (Ephesians 2:10).

During their abode in the Garden of Eden, God introduced Adam and Eve to the fundamental principles of stewardship. They understood the principle of the sovereignty of God (Genesis 1:27), since He was their Creator. Secondly, they were assigned as stewards or managers of God's property (Genesis 1:28, 29; Genesis 2:15). Finally, to help them understand the principle of reserving for God a portion of what they had been given, He instructed them that they had access to all but one of the trees in the Garden (Genesis 2:16, 17). The tree of the knowledge of good and evil was the one tree that they were to reserve for God, since it was His portion.

Sin Enters Into a Perfect World

Adam and Eve struggled with the stewardship principle that pertained to reserving a portion of what they had been given for God; they selfishly desired to have it all.

> *And the LORD God commanded the man, saying, "Of every tree of the garden you may freely eat; but of the tree of the knowledge of good and evil you shall not eat, for in the day that you eat of it you shall surely die.*
>
> Genesis 2:16, 17

Adam and Eve disobeyed God and ate of the fruit from the forbidden tree. They failed to return to God the portion that was due to Him. The result of their action was immediate and disastrous for the human race. As a result of their disobedience to God's command, sin entered into the world and God evicted them from the Garden (Genesis 3: 23, 24). They were no longer able to communicate directly with God, and could no longer bear to see His face, for they would have been destroyed by His glory.

When Adam and Eve disobeyed God's command, they demonstrated disregard for His principles of stewardship. This tendency was passed onto the entire human race (Romans 5:12). It is therefore no surprise that we find ourselves today struggling to adhere to God's principles of true stewardship. They also traded their perfect nature for a sinful one, which resulted in their separation from God (Isaiah 59:2). When we fail to follow God's principles of stewardship, our actions result in our separation from Him. That is not what God intended when He created the human race.

Once sin entered into the world, God's plan to redeem man back to Him became engaged. If the separation never occurred, through Adam and Eve's sin, then there would not have been a need for our redemption. Once the plan of redemption became engaged, God's principles of stewardship took on a deeper and more profound spiritual significance for the human race.

The Beginning of God's System of Stewardship – The When

Life for Adam and Eve continued after they were evicted from the Garden of Eden, but it was never the same for them. God blessed them with their first children, Cain and Abel.

> *And in the process of time it came to pass that Cain brought an offering of the fruit of the ground to the LORD. Abel also brought of the firstborn of his flock and of their fat. And the LORD respected Abel and his offering.*
>
> Genesis 4:3, 4

This is the first recorded instance in the Bible of an act of worship that included the offering of a sacrifice to God, and it occurred after Adam and Eve left the Garden of Eden. What is the significance of this to stewardship? Before Adam and Eve were evicted from the Garden of Eden, here were some highlights of their lives:

- They were close to God and He was close to them.
- They communicated with God face to face.
- They were perfect.
- No offerings or sacrifices to God were made or required in the Garden of Eden.

After they sinned and were evicted from the Garden of Eden:

- They were no longer close to God.
- God couldn't communicate with them face to face.
- They were no longer perfect.
- Because of their sin, the entire human race became sinners.
- God's plan of redemption became engaged.
- Their children made the first recorded instance of an offering or sacrifice to God (Genesis 4:3, 4).

According to Rabbi Samson Raphael Hirsch: a "sacrifice" implies giving up something that is of value to oneself for the benefit of another. An "offering" implies a gift which satisfies the receiver. The Almighty does not need our gifts. He has no needs or desires. The Hebrew word (for sacrifice) is **korban**, which is best translated as a means of bringing oneself into a closer relationship with the Almighty. The offering of **korbanot** was only for our benefit to come close to the Almighty. [2]

Adam and Eve's sin in the Garden of Eden separated the entire human race from God. Once sin entered into the world, the system of stewardship took on new spiritual significance; it provided a mechanism to allow the human race to come close to God.

The Spiritual Meaning of God's System of Stewardship – The Why

God implemented His system of stewardship in two (2) phases. The first phase was implemented prior to sin entering into the world and provided the following for the human race:

- It reinforced the sovereignty of God in the mind of man (Genesis 1:1, 27, 31).
- It reinforced God's ownership of everything that man acquired. We are the managers of God's property (Genesis 1:28; 2:15).
- It helped man understand the concept of reserving a portion for God (Genesis 2:16, 17).
- It demonstrated God's care and affection for the human race (Genesis 2:18).

The second phase was initiated after sin entered into the world and the human race became separated from God. During this phase He expanded the principles of stewardship to provide the following:

- A mechanism to allow the human race to come close to God (Genesis 4:3, 4).
- A reminder to us of our need to come close to Him.
- A mechanism to reveal to us His plan of redemption (John 3:16).
- A reaffirmation of His love for us - Christ's death was the ultimate sacrifice (Jeremiah 31:3).

Even though sin separated the human race from God, it has always been His desire to restore the relationship with us back to its pre-sin state. Why does God want us to come close to Him? Why would He spend so much effort on a race that had disobeyed Him? The principles of stewardship provide an answer to these questions. Listed in the sections below are some reasons why God implemented stewardship.

1. God Implemented Stewardship Because He Loves Us

In Jeremiah 31:3 the Bible describes the love of God for us,
The LORD has appeared of old to me, saying: "Yes,
I have loved you with an everlasting love; Therefore
with loving kindness I have drawn you."

Because of His great love for us, God desires that we come close to Him; He went to great lengths to implement His system of stewardship to reinforce that in our minds. Jesus spoke of the depth and breadth of His love for the human race, *"Greater love has no one than this, than to lay down one's life for his friends"* (John 15:13). Our human minds cannot begin to comprehend the everlasting love of God. However, when we adhere to His principles of stewardship in our lives, the Holy Spirit helps us comprehend His munificent love.

2. God Implemented Stewardship to Serve as a Reminder to Us

One of the frailties of human nature is its tendency to forget. Some people tie a string around a finger to help them remember, but they look at it later and say, "Aha, I have a string on my finger," but they cannot remember why. It is a natural human tendency to forget things.

The American Institute for Cognitive Therapy (AICT) states:
No one is exactly sure how memory works. We understand that the mind can store a tremendous amount of information—far more than any of us is capable of thinking about in a given moment. Having information in our minds, however, doesn't always mean having access to it. We've all experienced moments when we're certain we know something but are unable to remember it. Scientists have

given the sensation a name: Tip-of-the-Tongue phenomenon. It's in this category—things we know but can't remember—that mental blocks originate. We walk into a room and forget why we came; leave keys in the front door; make a call and draw a blank on the person we've dialed. None of this is unusual.

According to Judith Beck, a psychologist at the Center for Cognitive Therapy at the University of Pennsylvania, "Most of us are trying to juggle so much; it's no surprise that we become confused."

The AICT advises that the first step towards coping with anxiety from mental blocks is to anticipate it, and the second step is to prepare for it. Since God created us He knew of our tendency to forget, so He took the first step for us; He anticipated the anxieties of a sinful world. Secondly, in order to minimize our anxiety He gave us His principles of stewardship to serve as reminders of His love and His plan of redemption for us; God prepared us.

Whenever we bring our gifts to the altar, they should remind us that we are in need of being close to God. Paul understood the concept of being close to God; he characterized it as been crucified with Christ (Galatians 2:20).

Adam and Eve were the first stewards. The tree in the midst of the Garden of Eden was placed there by God to constantly remind them of His presence in their midst. When we practice the principles of stewardship in our lives, it serves as a reminder to us of God's presence in our lives. Just as the tree was physically in the middle of the Garden, stewardship puts God in the middle of our lives; it allows Him to become the epicenter of our very existence (Acts 17:28).

3. God Implemented Stewardship as a Test of Our Obedience

God created man with the freedom of choice and He empowered Adam and Eve to manage His entire creation. They were even allowed to name all the things that God created. However, He gave them one small test of their loyalty to Him, the tree of the knowledge of Good and Evil. They were not permitted to eat of the fruit of that one tree. It was a test of their obedience to Him and would prove their trustworthiness as stewards.

As faithful stewards, they were required to respect that tree as God's portion. If they chose to obey His command they would become co-owners of the world with God, but if they chose to disobey they would lose everything. Adam and Eve chose to disobey God by coveting His portion; they failed the test of obedience. They proved their untrustworthiness as stewards and lost all that had been given to them.

God has blessed us with lots of things: families, friends that care, homes, cars, good jobs, disposable income, freedom to worship, health and a sound mind, just to name a few. He has asked that we return the first portion to Him (Exodus 23: 19). If we choose to obey and demonstrate our trustworthiness as stewards, He has promised to multiply what we already possess beyond our wildest imaginations (Deuteronomy 12: 5-7, Proverbs 3: 9-10, Malachi 3:10, 2 Corinthians 9: 6-8). However, if we choose to disobey and prove to be untrustworthy stewards, we stand to lose everything (Haggai 1:5,6). The New Living Translation Bible brings this point home in a very sobering way;

> *This is what the LORD Almighty says: Consider how things are going for you! You have planted much but harvested little. You have food to eat, but not enough to fill you up. You have wine to drink, but not enough to satisfy your thirst. You have clothing to wear, but not enough to keep you warm. Your wages disappear as though you were putting them in pockets filled with holes!*

4. God Implemented Stewardship to Help Us Understand the Ugliness of Sin

The system of stewardship was implemented for man and not for God. God hates sin, but He loves the sinner. In Hebrews 1:9 the Bible explains that, *"You have loved righteousness and hated lawlessness;"*

Sin is very displeasing and repugnant to God. Ever since our first parents (Adam and Eve) sinned, our human nature has inherited a dispensation to sin and we fail to comprehend how displeasing sin is in the sight of God.

We often consider the really bad disgusting sins to be things like murder and rape, but the Bible does not support that human perspective on sin. In 1 John 5:17 the Bible states, *"All unrighteousness is sin"*. Each and every sin is despicable in the sight of God, and He uses the system of stewardship to help us understand the ugliness of sin in His sight.

When Adam, according to God's special directions, made an offering for sin, it was to him a most painful ceremony. His hand must be raised to take life, which God alone could give, and make an offering for sin. It was the first time he had witnessed death. As he looked upon the bleeding victim, writhing in the agonies of death, he was to look forward by faith to the Son of God, whom the victim prefigured, who was to die man's sacrifice.

This ceremonial offering, ordained of God, was to be a perpetual reminder to Adam of his guilt, and also a penitential acknowledgment of his sin. This act of taking life gave Adam a deeper and more perfect sense of his transgression, which nothing less than the death of God's dear Son could expiate. He marveled at the infinite goodness and matchless love, which would give such a ransom to save the guilty. As Adam was slaying the innocent victim, it seemed to him that he was shedding the blood of the Son of God by his own hand. He knew that if he had remained steadfast to God, and true to His holy law, there would have been no death of beast or of man. Yet in the sacrificial offerings, pointing to the great and perfect offering of God's dear Son, there appeared a star of hope to illuminate the dark and terrible future, and relieve it of its utter hopelessness and ruin.[3]

The system of stewardship that was presented to the Israelites consisted of a number of offerings, which are explained in further details in Chapter Five. Some of these sacrifices involved the killing of animals and the burning and eating of some of their entrails. The process of preparing and killing an animal for sacrifice was a very unnatural and unpleasant one for the worshipper as well as the onlookers. A visit to an animal slaughterhouse would help one to better understand how unpleasant this process of animal sacrificing was. The gruesome sight of an animal resisting being killed in preparation for sacrifice was meant to leave an indelible impression in the minds of the individual and the beholders that their sins were displeasing to God. The process of preparing the sacrifice was meant to present a powerful visual deterrent to the individual against continuing to practice sin.

5. God Implemented Stewardship to Reveal to Us His Plan of Redemption

God implemented the system of stewardship to reveal to us His plan of redemption for us. Because of the sins of Adam and Eve in the Garden of Eden, redemption for the entire human race became necessary.

The Bible states in Hebrews 9:22:

> *And according to the law almost all things are purified with blood, and without shedding of blood there is no remission.*

The plan of redemption required the shedding of blood. The redemption process was defined by God before the foundation of the world (1 Peter 1:19-21), but only became engaged after sin entered the world. In order for the human race to have a better understanding and appreciation of the process of redemption, God instituted the process of stewardship. One of the mandatory offerings required the repentant individual to bring to the altar an animal sacrifice. The animal sacrifice required the shedding of blood and was a sin offering from the repentant sinner to God. The sacrifices offered to God typified the ultimate sacrifice of Christ on the cross at Calvary for the redemption of the entire human race (John 17:3).

Prior to the death of Christ at Calvary, the process of presenting a sin offering to God allowed the individual to demonstrate his or her faith in the coming of Christ and their acceptance of the significance of His death. Matthew 1:21:

> *And she will bring forth a Son, and you shall call*
> *His name JESUS, for He will save His people from*
> *their sins.*

The coming of Christ and His death on the cross meant that we are no longer required to bring animal sacrifices to the altar (Ephesians 5:2). We read in Hebrews 7:27:

> *who does not need daily, as those high priests, to*
> *offer up sacrifices, first for His own sins and then for*
> *the people's, for this He did once for all when He*
> *offered up Himself.*

Under the old covenant, which existed prior to the death of Christ on the cross, animal sacrifices were required. Under the new covenant, which became effective after the death of Christ, our sacrifices now take on a completely different symbolism and meaning. Every time we bring our offering or sacrifice to the altar, it demonstrates our acceptance of Christ's death on the cross for us and publicly indicates our belief that He is the atoning lamb who "taketh away the sins of the world."

He paid the price for you and me so that we could gain eternal life; that's the result of God's sacrifice and the significance of stewardship to us.

6. God Implemented Stewardship as a Mechanism to Communicate His Thoughts

When Adam and Eve sinned, the lines of direct communication with God became disrupted. As a result of sin, God cannot communicate directly with man. There are times when by our very actions we signal to God that we do not wish to communicate with Him. The children of Israel refused to communicate with God and delegated that responsibility to Moses. When God implemented His system of stewardship, He desired that by our adherence to its original principles we would glimpse some of His deep thoughts of His love for us and His plan of redemption. We are always on God's mind (Jeremiah 29:11).

When we adhere to the principles of stewardship, God elevates our minds to understand His love for us and He reveals His secret thought to us. Communication is a two-way process; God to us and we to Him. Through our observance of God's principles of stewardship, we open up the channels of communication with Him. When we become faithful stewards, we communicate to God our acceptance of His love, our belief and acceptance of the death of Christ as the atoning lamb; we express our love for Him and our desire to be with Him when He returns.

Final Thoughts

When God created Adam and Eve they were perfect and close to Him; they were faithful stewards. Because they allowed the devil to encourage them to covet God's portion, the tree of knowledge of Good and Evil, they became unfaithful stewards. As a result of this, they displeased God.

An important spiritual significance of stewardship is that God instituted it to remind us of His everlasting love for us, and of our need to return to Him.

The practice of the principles of stewardship in the life of the individual helps him or her to understand how detestable sin is in the sight of God. By being a faithful steward, we allow the Holy Spirit to remind us that our sins displease God and they led to the death of His son.

The decision to adhere to God's principles of stewardship is a voluntary one. We decide our destiny: *"choose for yourselves this day whom you will serve"* (Joshua 24:15). Our decision to follow these principles demonstrates our love for God.

References

1. Hebrew #2896 – *Strong's Dictionary of Hebrew and Greek Words*
2. *Shabbat Shalom Weekly – Vayikra 5762, Torah Portion: Vayikra* by Rabbi Kalman Packouz
3. *"The Sacrificial Offering", The Story of Redemption* by Ellen G. White

Therefore, as through one man's offense judgment came to all men, resulting in condemnation, even so through one Man's righteous act the free gift came to all men, resulting in justification of life.

Romans 5:18

2

Stewardship as an Evangelical Tool

One of the biggest shortcomings of most stewardship programs is the failure to make the connection between God's system of stewardship, and His plan of salvation. This is unfortunate especially when we are given a divine charge: *And He said to them, "Go into all the world and preach the gospel to every creature* (Mark 16:15).

God has given us a mandate to be diligent in spreading His message of salvation — the good news of the gospel. Using the word of God as our guide, let us biblically establish the connection between God's system of stewardship and His plan of salvation for mankind.

The Commandment From God

In the Garden of Eden, God gave Adam and Eve a very simple command, *"of the tree of the knowledge of good and evil you shall not eat"* (Genesis 2:17).

Since Adam and Eve were created in the image and likeness of God (Genesis 1:27), there existed a very close relationship between He and them prior to the introduction of sin. God spoke directly to man and man to Him; there was direct communion and fellowship between man and God. This is illustrated below.

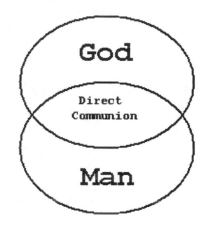

Garden of Eden - Prior to Sin

They were provided with everything that they needed. Not only was the direct communication between God and man active, but also the communication between man and woman was impeccable.

The Sin Against God

Sin is simply defined as disobedience to God's commandment. If God says to you that you should stop smoking and you continue to smoke, then you have disobeyed His command to you. Whenever we disobey the word of God, we sin against God (1 John 3:4).

The sin that Adam and Eve committed was that they disobeyed God and ate fruit from the tree that He forbade them to; it wasn't the fruit, it was the act.

The Consequences of Sin – The Penalty

Because of the devil and sin, Adam and Eve fell from their perfect condition and lost favor with God. They became separated from God and He could no longer communicate face to face with them. The diagram below demonstrates the effect of sin on the relationship between God and man.

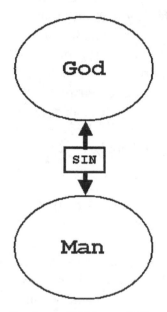

Garden of Eden – After Sin

God warns us that He is unable to answer our prayers because our sins have separated us from Him (Isaiah 59:1,2).

Now let us revisit the Garden of Eden one more time to gain a deeper understanding of what transpired during the infamous debate between man and the devil. When God told Adam and Eve: *"but of the tree of the knowledge of good and evil you shall not eat, for in the day that you eat of it you shall surely die"* (Genesis 2:17). God was actually saying to them, "If you disobey My command and eat fruit from the forbidden tree, you will become separated from Me." When we become separated from God, we become spiritually dead.

But the cunning serpent suggested to Eve that if she ate from the tree she would become closer to God. He elaborated, "So close, that you would become exactly like Him, knowing all that He knows." He subtly suggested to Adam and Eve that in order for them to be complete they needed to acquire God's portion for themselves. The devil had tried this before and he was cast out of heaven; Adam and Eve tried it and they were cast out of their paradise home.

Too often we fall prey to such a vain philosophy; we often reason that if we had a few more hours in the day, we could squeeze some time from our busy schedules to use our talents to the honor and glory of God. God gave us the principles of stewardship to protect us against becoming victims to such deceptive schemes of our arch enemy and to help us better manage our resources so that we do find time to use our talents to benefit others. If God had not made the time in His universal schedule to breathe into a pile of clay, then you and me would not have come into existence.

The Pardon for Sin – a Gift From God to Man

The Bible says in (Numbers 23:19): *God is not a man that He should lie.* So once sin entered the world, the sentence was pronounced on man – "the wages of sin is death" (Romans 6:23). But God had a plan to restore us back to our original sinless state, and He gave us the principles of stewardship to be a mechanism to help us understand His divine plan of redemption and restoration for the human race. He wants us to understand His plan of salvation to enable us to reveal it to the world (Matthew 28:19, 20). We can't proclaim the plan of redemption if we don't understand it.

Because of God's love for us, He substituted His son to die in our place. He couldn't change or commute the sentence, for the devil would have accused Him of being a liar and of showing favoritism to the human race (Satan was not spared the sentence when he rebelled against God, Isaiah 14:12-15). Secondly, Romans 6:23 would not be true. He offered His Son, Jesus, to pay the price for our sins. The apostle Paul in Romans 5:7,8 identifies Christ as the substitute for us. The penalty for our sins was enacted on Christ.

God taught this to ancient Israel using the types and symbols of the Levitical system of offerings. He teaches us, modern Israel, the same lessons using the principle of sacrificial giving, which is a very important aspect of stewardship.

Christ's death on the cross of Calvary restored the communication gap between God and man. This is visually represented below.

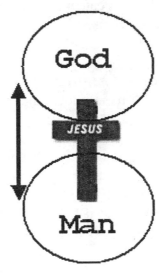

Restoration

Embedded in the principles of stewardship is God's plan of salvation and restoration for the human race. It points to the role of Christ as the ultimate sacrifice and the mediator between God and man. By following these principles in our lives, we allow God to enter into communion with us, and we allow the Holy Spirit to initiate the process of sanctification and restoration in us.

Here, clearly, is a manifestation of the hope we have in Jesus. No matter our obedience in our works, no matter how faithful we live, no matter how much fruit we bear to the glory of God, none of us can ever stand before God, ourselves, unblamable and unreprovable in His sight. That is why we have Jesus, who, through His life and death, presents us in the spotless robe of His righteousness, the only righteousness that is indeed "unblameable and unreprovable." This righteousness is ours—by faith alone.[1]

Once sin entered into the world and the direct line of communication between God and man became severed, God was no longer our main focus. Therefore, He used alternative methods to capture our attention and to communicate with us. Stewardship was one of those alternative methods He used.

The devil tells us that we are lost forever, we are too sinful and we would never be able to get back to God. He tries to convince us that God is a harsh God – "one strike and you're out." The principles of stewardship assist us in understanding God's mercy, long-suffering and patience towards us.

The sacrifices of the Levitical system of offerings all pointed to Christ's death on the cross. He was the only one capable of bearing the sins of the world. Christ's sacrifice arose as a sweet smelling savor unto God (Matthew 3:16), and it revealed His love for us. Our sacrifices of our time, talent and possessions reveal our love for others (John 13:35, 1 Peter 4:10). Our acts of stewardship don't save us, but we can't be saved without acts of stewardship (James 2:18, 20, 26).

The Jerusalem principle: use Christian stewardship to address major challenges and problems dividing God's people. Stewardship can destroy problems between Christians that logic, reasoning, and discussion do not address.

People problems produce the most immediate, stressful challenges to Christian stewardship. People problems are life's primary source for stress. Being God's people among people who choose to reject God results in stressful situations. Christians have opportunity to be merciful because people wrong us. Christians have opportunity to love our enemies because some people are enemies. Christians have opportunity to reject vengeance because some people are unjust to us. Christians have opportunity to forgive because some people sin against us. Jesus said, if we only love those who love us or greet those who greet us, we behave precisely as godless people behave (Matthew 5:46,47).

God uses Christian stewardship to heal sickness in human relationships. What sickness? [The sicknesses of: prejudice, arrogance, attitudes of superiority, attitudes of condescension, and rejection.] God's love is demonstrated powerfully through the human acts of Christian stewardship.

When Christianity began in Acts 2, only Jews or Jewish converts became Christians. Early in Christianity, Jewish Christians regarded Christianity as a Jewish religious movement that fulfilled God's promise to Israel. The earliest Christians understanding of Jesus' great commission (was) "take the gospel to all the Jews scattered throughout the world."

The baptism of non-Jewish people who believed in Jesus Christ created a major crisis. First, the initial reaction of Jewish Christians to the conversion of people who were not Jewish was this: it is improper and inappropriate to include such people in the Christian community (Acts 11:1-3). Second, some Jewish Christians insisted that people who were not Jews could become Christians only if they observed Jewish customs and requirements (Acts 15:1,5).

What a barrier between Christians in God's family! God's community could never become the people God wanted as long as that barrier existed. Christian alienation could never achieve God's purposes. God removed the barrier (Ephesians 2:11-22), but many Christians did not.

Christian stewardship assaulted the barrier.[2]

Before Mount Calvary

Prior to the death of Christ on Mount Calvary, the sacrifices offered by the repentant sinner symbolized Christ's death on the cross. His death was the ultimate sacrifice. During this period of Christianity, the believers were looking back to the fall of Adam and Eve in the Garden of Eden and forward to the first coming of Christ and His death on the cross.

Prior to the events on Mount Calvary, one of the important lessons conveyed to the worshipper by God's principles of stewardship was that the individual was a sinner in need of a savior. As the individual followed these principles, he or she demonstrated to God his or her belief in the blessed hope of the coming of the Messiah (Isaiah 7:14, Matthew 1:21). They also demonstrated to God that He was the epicenter of their lives.

Prior to the death of Christ on the cross, the principles of stewardship were used by God to demonstrate to the Israelites His plan of redemption, which they were to reveal to the world. These principles also served as a reminder to them that they needed to come back to Him. As they made these principles a part of their daily lives, it etched in their minds God's love for them (John 3:16).

After Mount Calvary

Christ's death on the cross of Calvary abolished the need for the sacrifice of lambs, bullocks, fruits, grain and doves on the physical altar. Christ's death changed the nature of the sacrifice, but it did not abolish the need for stewardship. Today our sacrifices unto God consist of our time, talents, possessions and our lives. We are still required to present our sacrifices to God, because we are still sinners in need of a savior (Romans 3:23).

God's principles of stewardship must remain active in our lives if we are to be saved. During this period of Christianity, we are looking back at the death of Christ at the cross and forward to His second coming. Therefore, to us, God's system of stewardship takes on a whole new meaning. After Christ's death, our sacrificial gifts to God signify:

- Our belief in His death as our atoning sacrifice.
- Our acceptance and belief in His plan of salvation as the only way by which we can be saved (Acts 4:12).

- Our acceptance of His role as savior in our lives.
- Our acceptance of Him as Lord of our lives.
- Our understanding and appreciation of His wonderful love for us.
- Our desire to come close to God.
- Our belief in His imminent return.

When we voluntarily (2 Corinthians 9:7) follow God's principles of stewardship, we symbolically exchange our material gifts for the gift of eternal life. It is not the act of following the principles of stewardship that saves us; it is our belief that we are saved and our love for God that motivates us to follow the principles of stewardship. In response to our acts of love to Him, and to one another, God accepts our sacrifice as a sweet smelling savor. This is the spiritual link between His plan of salvation and His system of stewardship. It is a spiritual link that must be experienced by the individual; it allows that person to become close to God while living here on earth. The practice of stewardship in the life of the individual must be motivated by his or her love for God and their fellow man if that individual is to be saved.

My Practice of True Stewardship Guarantees My Salvation

One night a rich young man approached Jesus inquiring how he might be saved (Matthew 19:16-22). Jesus advised the man to keep the commandments. That was something that the young man boasted to his credit. He was a law-abiding Christian, but he felt a lack of fulfillment and completeness in his life. He sought Christ's help in fulfilling this void in his life. Christ said to him, *"If you want to be perfect, go, sell what you have and give to the poor, and you will have treasure in heaven; and come, follow Me"* (Matthew 19:21). The rich young ruler reflected on his great wealth and felt that it was too critical to his financial well-being and social status to give up. After all, he had spent a lifetime acquiring his fortunes, how could he give all that up overnight? This was one commandment from God that he simply couldn't obey. He left the presence of God a sad and empty person; he chose his wealth over his personal salvation.

This man desired to be saved and he had observed the commandments of God all of his life, but he realized that something was missing from his Christian experience. The Greek word for perfect in verse 21 is **teleios**[3]; it means becoming mature, whole, or complete. It describes the heart that is turned wholly towards God, the life that has been given entirely to the Father, Son, and Holy Spirit.

God got straight to the point and identified to the rich young man the reason why he hadn't achieved completeness in his Christian experience. He was lacking in one critical area; he hadn't been a faithful steward. Based on this man's knowledge of the Scriptures, it could be concluded that he was aware of the principles of true stewardship, but he had not practiced them in his life. He had focused on the things he felt were important to his Christianity, but he still wasn't complete. This man was a ruler. He was asked to become humble, so that others could benefit; He was asked to do unto others as Christ did for Him. Christ became abased, so that we might become elevated (2 Corinthians 8:9). Christ was attempting to teach this man that fulfillment in the Christian experience can't be achieved without adherence to the principles of stewardship.

Stewardship allows us to come closer to God as we offer our sacrifices (talents, time, and possessions) to Him; it allows us to experience completeness and fulfillment in our Christian experience because we benefit others. God identified to the rich young man that his possessions were getting in the way of his salvation; they were separating him from God. He needed to rid himself of them before he could come close to God. Whatever is separating you and me from God must be eliminated from our lives if we are to inherit eternal life (Romans 8:39). When we allow the Holy Spirit to weave the principles of stewardship into the fabric of our daily lives, it eliminates the things that separate us from God; as a result we are drawn closer to Him.

The key word God used in explaining stewardship to the rich young ruler was "give". Giving is the cornerstone of stewardship. God did not tell him to go sell everything he had and keep the profits;

instead he was told to give it all to the poor. He was told to practice the most crucial principle of true stewardship – giving to God so that He might use our gifts (consume them as a sweet smelling savor) to benefit others. This proved too difficult a challenge for the ruler. If he had depended on the Holy Spirit rather than on his works of righteousness, he would have been saved.

> It ought also to be observed, that he does not only enjoin him to sell, but likewise to give to the poor; for to part with riches would not be in itself a virtue, but rather a vain ambition. Profane historians applaud Crates, a Theban, because he threw into the sea his money and all that he reckoned valuable; for he did not think that he could save himself unless his wealth were lost; as if it would not have been better to bestow on others what he imagined to be more than he needed. Certainly, as charity is the bond of perfection (Colossians 3:14), he who deprives others, along with himself, of the use of money, deserves no praise; and therefore Christ applauds not simply the selling but liberality in assisting the poor.
>
> The mortification of the flesh is still more strongly urged by Christ, when He says, "Follow me."[4]

Our understanding of the principles of true stewardship is critical to our salvation. Our adherence to those principles determines our eligibility for eternal life.

Final Thoughts

Adam was the first man who ever walked upon the earth. He was created in the image and likeness of God; therefore, he represented you and me as mankind. God created Adam and Eve in a perfect state, and placed them in the perfect home — the Garden of Eden. Not only did sin enter into the world by the acts of one man, but also by the offence of that one man, judgment came upon all men (Romans 5:12, 18).

Christ came and He paid the penalty for our sins. This is the good news of the gospel. God is such a God of love; we may never fully understand why He went through all that He did to demonstrate His love for us and to redeem us back to Him.

When God implemented His system of stewardship, it was designed to reveal to us His plan of salvation so that we could reveal it to a world in sin. It was also given to assist us in understanding how disgusting sin is in His sight. Our practice of the true principles of stewardship, motivated by our love for God, is necessary if we are to achieve eternal life.

References:

1. *Living The Advent Hope* (Adult Sabbath School Bible Study Guide Fourth Quarter 2002 published by the General Conference of Seventh-day Adventist.)
2. *The "Jerusalem Principle" of Stewardship Lesson Eight* - David Chadwell & West-Ark Church of Christ
3. Greek #5046 – *Strong's Dictionary of Hebrew and Greek Words*
4. *Commentary on Matthew, Mark, Luke - Volume 2* by Johm Calvin, 1509-1564

For God so loved the world that He gave His only begotten Son, that whoever believes in Him should not perish but have everlasting life.

John 3:16

3

Stewardship – It's All About Love

God is love. If He ever ceases to love us, then He would cease to be God. His very nature is love. Everything we do for God and with God must be motivated by our love for Him and for others. Jesus said that in addition to loving Him, we must love our neighbor (Luke 10:27). If we say we love God but we are feuding with our neighbor, then we do not love God. Stewardship is love in action. God loves us, so He gave His son to die in our place (John 3:16). If we love God and our neighbor, we would return God's portion to Him, which He uses to bless our neighbor; when our neighbor, who loves God and us, returns His portion, He uses it to bless us. This completes the circle of love.

After Adam and Eve were evicted from the Garden of Eden and they came to the full realization of the consequences of their act of disobedience, they were devastated. Were you ever lied to by a smooth talking individual, and found yourself committing your resources only to discover that it was all a lie? Do you remember how you felt after that experience? Now you can begin to appreciate how Adam and Eve felt after their encounter with the devil. Let me share with you an incident of deception in my life that initially was very devastating, but it later helped me understand how Adam and Eve could have possibly felt after they were thrown out of the Garden of Eden – the Garden of Delight.

When I first arrived in the United States of America, I brought all of the money I saved over the years with me. I arrived in New York eager to begin my degree program. One Sunday afternoon I decided to discover lower Manhattan and to visit the stores that sold electronic equipment. While strolling the sidewalk, I was approached by a man who invited me to step over to his "pavement store" to view some electronic items. He spoke very smoothly and proceeded to arouse my interest in a video camera. As he talked about the features of the camera, I began to envision myself making videos of the scenery of the city and sending them back home for my mom to see and enjoy.

I informed the man that I needed to travel to Brooklyn to get some more cash. He offered to take the ride back to Brooklyn with me and bring along the camera so that no one would purchase it before I had a chance to return with the cash. I thought that offer was very thoughtful of him. On the train ride back to Brooklyn, I continued to conjure up in my mind images of me capturing note-worthy events on film such as my graduation from college.

At last the moment arrived. I retrieved the cash and traded it for the beautiful shiny new box. The man disappeared with the cash. After catching my breath from all the excitement and anticipation, I began to open the box. I removed layer after layer of wrapping paper for what seemed like an eternity. Anticipation gave way to anxiety; in the quiet of the dining room I could hear my heart pound louder and louder against my chest. Finally, I removed the last layer of wrapping material; there in the center of the box was a single large stone. For several seconds I stared in dismay and horror, before I came to the realization of what had just transpired. I dashed out of the house and ran all the way to the train station, but the man was nowhere to be found.

I had traded a significant part of my savings for "nothing". I felt dismayed, like a fool, angry; I wish I had never gone to lower Manhattan that day. For weeks after that incident, I just couldn't imagine how I could have allowed myself to be deceived like that; I had neglected advice from my friends and family: "beware of the guys selling stuff on the sidewalks", they warned. It took me a while to get over the feeling of shame and betrayal. How could I tell my friends what had happened to me? They would laugh at me and think that I was stupid. It took me years before I was able to speak about that experience without feeling the pain and the shame. Only after I began to understand the spiritual significance of that experience, was I able to share it with others.

For me it was only part of my tuition fees, but for Adam and Eve it was their life and that of the entire human race. Imagine the devastation, the dismay, and the guilt and anguish that Adam and Eve felt after they realized that Satan had deceived them. They lost their home and freedom to become slaves to sin. They traded their perfect life, their perfect environment and their affinity to God for "nothing". They traded paradise for prison.

Not only did they make a terrible mistake in their lives, but also the entire human race had now become estranged from God. In the process they also incurred the curse of sin. God needed to reach out to Adam and Eve; He needed to reassure them and to remind them He still loved them and He hadn't turned his back on them. God wanted to show them He had a plan for them. He wanted to help them restore their confidence in something and in someone. In their moment of deepest despair, God intervened to show them His love. God had a plan that one day would reunite them and the entire human race with Him.

Up until this point in their existence, Adam and Eve had been practicing the principles of stewardship because they were assigned to manage (as stewards) God's property. Once they found themselves outside of the Garden of Eden, stewardship took on a different perspective for them. They and their children now found themselves offering sacrifices to God, which was not a part of their daily routine during their stay in Eden.

This new stewardship experience was given to them by God to allow them to begin to understand that because of His love for them, He had provided a mechanism to redeem them from their fallen state. They began to learn the lesson of returning to God a portion of what they had earned, something they failed to understand in Eden. Equally as important is that the sacrifices they were bringing to the altar signified Christ who would one day die for the sins of everyone. They found themselves looking forward to the coming of the Lamb, without blemish, who would be sacrificed for the sins of the world (1 Peter 1:18-20); this gave them hope in their despair.

To better comprehend the meaning of true love, let us consider the four (4) Greek words for love:

Eros — is the word used for sensual or physical love. Eros was the Greek god of love. This word does not appear in the New Testament. It is the root of the English word erotic.

Stergo — means to feel affection, especially the affection between parents and children. It is also used for the affection of a people for their king or a dog for his master. It does not appear in the New Testament, except in compound form in Romans 12:10 (Philostorgos) where it is translated as "devoted." The negative form (astorgos) appears in Romans 1:31 ("heartless," "unloving") and 2 Timothy 3:3 ("without love," "unloving").

Phileo — is the general word for love and affection. It is used for attraction of people to one another without regard for family relationships, such as Philadelphia, the love of a friend or brother, a feeling as in 2 Peter 2:17. It is frequently used in compound forms and, as such, may be used for attraction to inanimate objects — Philosophia — the love of knowledge, Colossians 2:8.

Agape (noun) and **Agapao** (verb) — is the word reserved for Godly love. This special significance really comes in the New Testament period. Agape is not found in secular literature, at least to any great extent, during the biblical period. Agape is the only form of love that originates from God.

God Demonstrates His (Agape) Love to Man

During one of the lowest points in man's history, which began after the entrance of sin into the world, God continued to show His love towards Adam and Eve. The Bible says: *Now Adam knew Eve his wife, and she conceived and bore Cain, and said, "I have acquired a man from the LORD"* (Genesis 4:1). They continued to trust in the Lord and to look for demonstrations of His continued love for them. God used the system of stewardship to demonstrate to Adam and Eve, and to every human being who would follow, His everlasting love for the human race.

God implemented the system of stewardship for our benefit and not for His. We are the ones in need of a reminder of God's love and care for us. God's system of stewardship required the repentant sinner to bring a sacrificial offering to the altar. The act of offering the sacrificial gift on the altar symbolized the death of Christ on the cross of Calvary for the sins of the world. As we follow the principles of stewardship in our lives, the Holy Spirit reminds us that God has made a way of escape from the penalty of sin, because of His agape love for us. Christ paid the price when He willingly gave His life on the cross for our sins (John 19:33-35).

> While Jesus hung upon the cross, as the soldier pierced his side with a spear, there came out blood and water, in two distinct streams, one of blood, the other of clear water. The blood was to wash away the sins of those who should believe in His name. The water represents that living water which is obtained from Jesus to give life to the believer.[1]

The principles of stewardship reveal to us the reason why Christ gave Himself on the cross for our sins; it was because of God's agape love for His creations.

> As the soldier pierced that holy body, which had been dead already for some time, blood and water flowed forth. Now it is well known that blood will not flow from the body of any mere man. The moment the heart stops beating, the body grows cold, the blood coagulates and cannot possibly flow, because at death the body goes to corruption. But His body did not see corruption (Acts 2:27), and so the blood flowing from His pierced side tells us He was not a mere man, but God manifest in flesh. That's why the apostle John

alone records this miracle, for he tells us in chapter
20:31 that he wrote his gospel, not first of all that men
might believe in Jesus, but that they might believe
Who Jesus is, that "ye might believe that Jesus is the
Christ, the Son of God." Yes, the blood our Savior
sheds light as to Who He is; therefore the use of that
term "the blood of Christ."[2]

God's love for us was demonstrated to the entire world at
Calvary; it was Christ's sacrificial gift to God. During His life on
earth and even unto His death, Christ demonstrated His adherence
to the principles of stewardship. When He told His disciples that
they should give back to Caesar the things that are Caesar's and
give back to God the things that are God's (Matthew 22:21), He was
reinforcing the principles of stewardship in their minds.

Regardless of how high we may value the sacrifices that we
bring to the altar, they pale in comparison to the sacrifice made by
Christ on the cross for us. God's sacrifice was motivated by His
agape love for us; our sacrifices to Him should be motivated by our
agape love for Him. The Holy Spirit manifests the agape love of
God in our hearts, which allows us to become faithful stewards.

God gave us His firstborn, His best; we should give Him our
best. When the children of Israel rejected God's prophets, He did not
stop loving them. When you and me sin, He does not stop loving us.
We don't have to be lovable to be loved by God. One of the reasons
why God implemented His system of stewardship was to help us
understand how His love has saved us from the penalty of sin.

Since we live in the period following Christ's death on the
cross, whenever we honor God in the use of our time, possessions
and abilities, we reinforce in our minds our belief in the second
coming of Christ; He is "the King of King and Lord of Lords", who
will abolish sin and Satan forever (Hebrews 12:2).

We Have an Opportunity to Demonstrate Our (Agape) Love to God

Whenever love is understood and appreciated by the recipient, it evokes a response to the giver; that is the power of true love. When we fully understand and appreciate God's (agape) love for us, we will not find ourselves responding to Him with human (phileo) love; we will only respond with (agape) love. When the Holy Spirit enlightens our minds concerning God's love towards us, He motivates us to a holy response that is based on love; agape love restricts us from putting a value-limit on our gifts to God.

Stewardship is a test of our love towards God. When we are fully committed to the principles of stewardship, we no longer constantly monitor the clock when we come into His presence to worship Him; we no longer search the deep corners of our pockets or purses to find a dollar to put in the offering plate. Instead, we find ourselves planning our activities and budgets around God and not in spite of Him.

Let's prayerfully review a passage of Scripture recorded in Luke 7:36-47 to discover the lessons on stewardship:

> *Then one of the Pharisees asked Him to eat with him. And He went to the Pharisee's house, and sat down to eat. And behold, a woman in the city who was a sinner, when she knew that Jesus sat at the table in the Pharisee's house, brought an alabaster flask of fragrant oil, and stood at His feet behind Him weeping; and she began to wash His feet with her tears, and wiped them with the hair of her head; and she kissed His feet and anointed them with the fragrant oil. Now when the Pharisee who had invited Him saw this, he spoke to himself, saying, "This Man, if He were a prophet, would know who and what manner of woman this is who is touching Him, for she is a sinner." And Jesus answered and said to him, "Simon, I have something to say to you." So he said, "Teacher, say it."*
>
> *"There was a certain creditor who had two*

debtors. One owed five hundred denarii, and the other fifty. And when they had nothing with which to repay, he freely forgave them both. Tell Me, therefore, which of them will love him more?" Simon answered and said, "I suppose the one whom he forgave more." And He said to him, "You have rightly judged." Then He turned to the woman and said to Simon, "Do you see this woman? I entered your house; you gave me no water for My feet, but she has washed My feet with her tears and wiped them with the hair of her head. You gave me no kiss, but this woman has not ceased to kiss my feet since the time I came in. You did not anoint my head with oil, but this woman has anointed my feet with fragrant oil. Therefore I say to you, her sins, which are many, are forgiven, for she loved much. But to whom little is forgiven, the same loves little.

The narrative opens with a demonstration of God's love, since it was unthinkable for a Pharisee or a religious leader to visit the house of a leper; Jesus accepted the invitation, He never turns down an invitation from us (Revelation 3:20).

Luke does not mention her name nor does he record a single word spoken by the woman in her sacrificial act of stewardship. He notes that the woman was a sinner. It does not appear that Simon believed in Jesus or loved Jesus because he did not extend to Him the normal hospitality. Common courtesy for the day would have dictated that as soon as Jesus entered the house of Simon, He would have been greeted with a kiss, His feet would have been washed, and His head would have been anointed with oil. It appears that Simon carefully avoided every custom that would have made Jesus feel welcome.

When the Bible says *"when a woman"* it is literally translated from the Greek "And look a woman!" The shock was not only because of this woman's reputation, but also in those days it was not customary for women to be in the presence of the men gathered in a room. The women would have been off in another room. This woman's desire was to find Jesus and to bring her gift to His feet. She had encountered Jesus before and had understood His love and compassion for sinners. Her act of stewardship demonstrated her understanding and appreciation of God's love towards her.

An alabaster flask was made of soft stone to preserve the quality of the precious and expensive perfume. This woman had no value-limit on her sacrifice to God. It took a lot of courage for her to enter the room, knowing the customs of her day. In her act of stewardship, she was outwardly demonstrating her response to Jesus' love and compassion for sinners. She knew that she was a sinner, but she had encountered her savior; He was the One who would save her from her sins and change her life forever. Even though she never said a word her actions spoke voluminously.

She knelt at the feet of Jesus with the perfume she brought, intending to anoint His feet. But then she began to weep; she wept uncontrollably, her tears falling on Jesus' dusty feet. These were tears of joy and not of shame or sorrow. When we have a spiritual encounter with Jesus, there is great joy in our hearts and in heaven (Luke 15:7). She then began to kiss His feet; in fact the literal translation is "kiss His feet again and again". When we discover the agape love of God, there is no gift that is too large for us to bring to His feet. No act of human stewardship can match the act that Christ accomplished at Calvary because of His love for mankind. As the sweet fragrance of the precious oil filled the room, her sacrifice arose to God as a sweet aroma (Leviticus 3:16).

Everyone in the room became aware of her actions. All eyes were now focused on Jesus wondering what He would do. They reasoned in their minds that if He was really a prophet He would have rejected her actions, especially from this woman of such vain reputation. However, Jesus was well pleased with her sacrifice. Instead of rebuking the woman and rejecting her sacrifice, He rebuked her accusers.

When our acts of stewardship are motivated by agape love, God is always well pleased with them; our sacrifices arise unto Him as a sweet aroma. This woman's act of stewardship was at great personal cost. Not only did it cost the expensive vial of perfume (her most precious possession), but also at the time it cost her the humility of kissing, washing and drying the dirty feet of Christ with her hair. Perhaps the greatest cost she faced was the scorn and rejection of the self-righteous Pharisee and his dinner guests. This woman understood that everything she had belonged to God. She demonstrated her trustworthiness as a faithful steward.

Simon's reaction reveals that he had not as yet experienced the love of God in his life. He couldn't comprehend the woman's act of true stewardship. Since the Pharisee had not experienced God's agape love, he could not respond accordingly; he placed a value-limit on his response to God's love. Unlike the man in the story Jesus told, Simon did not realize that he could not repay the debt he owed.

If the other occupants in the room had realized they were in the very presence of the Almighty God or had experienced conversion in their hearts, they would have rushed to present their sacrifices at His feet. When an individual has not experienced the agape love of God in his or her life or true conversion in the heart, that individual cannot adhere to the principles of stewardship. More often than not the gift that is brought to the altar falls short, and the sacrifice does not arise as a sweet aroma to God.

Jesus again reiterated to this woman in the presence of her accusers (v47) that her many sins had been forgiven. She was already convinced of that, but He wanted to be sure that her accusers heard it again. It was because she realized that her sins were forgiven that she felt close to God, her offering (korban) was her way of acknowledging her freedom from the guilt and shame of her sins. She was now free to express her love for God. This was not phileo love; she expressed agape love.

This woman met many other men before she met Jesus, and they all had given her gifts in exchange for her services; they made her a slave to her sins. But when she encountered Jesus, He gave her external life in exchange for her sins; He liberated her from her sins (John 8:36). Only Jesus can forgive us of our sins and free us to love again, with an agape love. It doesn't matter how terrible you believe your sins are or how long you have been living in sin, only Jesus can free you from your sins (Isaiah 1:18). Only Jesus can give us the gift of eternal life; His death and resurrection provides a life-time warranty. By adhering to the principles of stewardship in our lives, we can achieve liberation from the sins of covetousness, guilt and greed.

God Uses Our Sacrifices to Benefit Others – Love Extended

As we read and understand the Levitical offerings, discussed in detail in Chapter 4, it becomes apparent that depending on the type of offering, either all or part of it was ultimately consumed by fire. Once it was consumed, the offering arose to God as a sweet savor.

The Hebrew word for fire in the Old Testament is *aysh*[3]. The word *aysh* can be further decomposed into two parts: "A", **aleph**, often refers to "God," and "Sh", **shin**, means "bringing forth, or birth." So the distilled definition for the word *aysh* (fire) could be rendered, "The birth of God in us" which occurs when Christ comes and makes His abode with us, or in our heart, through the Holy Ghost. Therefore, when God consumed the individual's sacrifice with fire (aysh), He signified to the repentant individual that his or her sins had been forgiven and he or she had experienced the birth of God within; the worshipper was once again close to Him.

In Luke 7:36-47, the woman actually presented her sacrifice to God. As the oil anointed Christ's feet, it was consumed and the fragrance arose to Him as a sweet savor. This signified that Christ had forgiven the woman's sin, and she had experienced the birth of God within. Every time we follow God's principles for true stewardship and bring our sacrifices to the altar, He still consumes our offering; these sacrifices can be in the form of our possessions, our time, our influence, or our talents. We, in turn, receive the birth of God in us.

When God consumes our offering today, there is no fire that comes down from heaven to burn up the offering plates at the altar. Perhaps, if God were to send fire down from heaven to consume our offerings at the altar, many of us would run out the building through the nearest exit door, or the deacons would quickly dowse the flames using a fire extinguisher, or someone in the congregation would use their cell phone to dial 911.

When God consumes our offering today, He uses it to further the spreading of the good news of salvation and to provide for the needs of someone we may never come to know. When He consumes our offering, we experience "the birth of God in us"; Christ comes and makes His abode with us, in our heart, through the Holy Ghost.

Final Thoughts

God's system of stewardship is founded on His agape love for us.

As the Father loved [agapao] Me, I also have loved [agapao] you; abide in My love [agape].

John 15:9

When God looked down through the ages of time and saw the negative effects that Adam and Eve's sin would bring to bear on the human race, He grieved for us (Genesis 6:6). The Hebrew word that is being used in this verse is **nacham**[4]. The meaning of **nacham** is explained by the phrase, "and it grieved Him at His heart." This provides us with a human insight into the pain that sin causes God. Sometimes we find ourselves enjoying our indulgence in sinful acts, but we must not let ourselves forget that sin is a dangerous thing. When we begin to understand the damage that sin can do to our lives and the lives of others, we learn to ask God to help us to stay in His love and to resist sin.

When we voluntarily bring our gifts to the altar and God finds them to be acceptable, just as He did in olden days, He "consumes" our gift at the altar. When God "consumes" our sacrifice, He uses it to meet the needs of others, thus allowing us to love our neighbor as He loved us.

Our motivation for observing God's system of stewardship must be His agape love. Only God can replace the eros, the stergo, and the phileo in our hearts with His agape love.

Agape love looks beyond the faults in the individual and sees the need. Therefore, when we were still in sin, God saw that we needed a savior and He sent His son to die on Calvary as the sacrifice for our sins. The phileo love looks beyond the needs of the individual and sees the faults. When the disciples saw the blind man (John 9:1-3), they immediately enquired of Christ *"Rabbi, who sinned, this man or his parents, that he was born blind?"* They looked beyond the need of the blind man and saw his sins. Sometimes instead of allowing God to use our abilities and possessions to help others, we chide those less fortunate than us because of their circumstances. Stewardship allows us to look beyond the faults of our neighbors in order to supply their needs, just as Christ did when He healed the blind man.

References:

1. *The Great Controversy* – 1858 Edition by Ellen G. White
2. Ibid
3. Hebrew #784 – *Strong's Dictionary of Hebrew and Greek Words*
4. Hebrew #5162 – *Strong's Dictionary of Hebrew and Greek Words*

But this Man, after He had offered one sacrifice for
sins forever, sat down at the right hand of God.
Hebrews 10:12

4

The Levitical System of Offerings: The Principles of Stewardship Revealed Part 1

The entrance of sin into the world did not catch God off-guard. God is omniscient (John 21:17); He knew when man was created, with the freedom of choice, exactly what man would do. Prior to creating man, He implemented a mechanism to deal with the consequences of sin (Titus 1:2).

During Adam and Eve's stay in the Garden of Eden, God implemented Phase I of His plan of stewardship. During this phase, He sought to teach them the different roles in the world. God was the creator and the provider and their roles were that of partners with Him and managers of His property. They were to be the model of faithful stewards. Once sin entered into the world, the plan of stewardship entered a new phase; Phase II focused on God as Savior and Redeemer of the world. The role of mankind had also changed since Adam and Eve were no longer partners but now only managers of God's property; they also acquired new roles as sinners in need of a savior. Because they failed the test of obedience in Eden, they could no longer be examples of perfect stewards; they now became teachers of the principles of stewardship to the rest of the world (beginning with their children). They would teach what God taught them.

One of the consequences of sin was a separation between God and man. A by-product of the separation was a disruption in the direct communication between God and man.

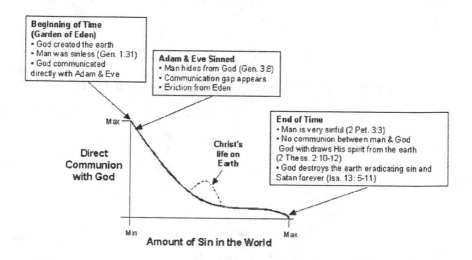

As the above diagrams shows, in the Garden of Eden, prior to sin, God and man were close and direct communion existed between man and God; no communication gap existed between God and the human race during that time. Once sin entered the world, Adam and Eve sought to distance themselves from God (Genesis 3: 8); the communication gap between God and the human race first appears. As the amount of sin in the world reaches its maximum, the direct communication between God and man ceases. Finally, sin becomes so pervasive and destructive to the fabric of human nature that God destroys the wicked, sin, the earth and Satan forever. The small spike on the graph is due to the presence of Christ on the earth. He was both God and man, so during His existence here on earth, there was a brief increase in the direct communion between God and man.

God implemented His system of stewardship to: help restore His image in us, re-establish communication with us, help us understand His love for us and, reveal to us His plan of salvation for the world. God system of stewardship was implemented for man and man only. In the beginning God created man in His own image and likeness (Hebrew word *tseh'-lem*[1] in Genesis 1:27). Translated more closely to the Hebrew, it would read, "Man was a reflection, as from a mirror, of God." The first man was called Adam; Adam = A + Dam.

> The letter Aleph(a) is the beginning of the Jewish alphabet. The aleph in Jewish theology is actually an expression of the image of Yahveh and is thus the Lord and Master of all the letters. The first (two) 2 letters of the alphabet spell father, (ba) ab or av meaning father. Man made in God's image. The second part of Adam's name "Dam" is from "Dom" meaning blood.[2]

All of mankind originated from Adam, including Eve. Once Adam and Eve sinned and they were thrown out of the Garden of Eden, they became separated from God. In order to comprehend the concept of separation from God, try this simple exercise. If you stand in front of a clean mirror, you see a reflection of yourself, but as you move further and further away from the mirror, your reflection gets smaller and smaller and more of the things around you appear in the mirror. The science of physics refers to this as the law of reflection, or the phenomenon of reflectivity. The law of reflection tells us that it is light rays from the source that are reflected by the mirror.

We are mirrors that reflect the light from the source of all light — God (Psalm 18:28). If you move backwards and far enough from the mirror, your image in the mirror becomes less conspicuous; the mirror becomes filled with images of the surrounding room. As man becomes more and more separated from God, His image in man becomes smaller and smaller. As we become separated from God, we reflect less and less of the light of God in our lives; more and more we begin to reflect the characteristics of the world. The principles of stewardship were given to us by God to assist us in staying connected with Him, thereby allowing us to reflect more and more Christ-like characteristics in our lives.

After Adam and Eve left the Garden of Eden, they were able to teach their children by word of mouth the principles of God and His system of stewardship. As generations progressed from Adam and Eve, the children of Israel, God's people, found themselves as slaves in Egypt. During their slavery in Egypt, the distance between the Israelites and God had grown quite significantly and His image in their minds was non-existent. The Israelites lost connection with God and began to worship the false gods of their Egyptian masters. All of God's principles were also lost. God's principles of stewardship were not transferred from generation to generation during the period of time while the Israelites were in bondage in Egypt. The Egyptians had succeeded in replacing the perception of God as the creator and provider in the Israelites' minds with that of their false gods. Naturally the Israelites had no desire to adhere to God's principles of stewardship. The fact that the principles of stewardship have withstood the test of time and adversity proves that they were spoken from the mouth of God.

God chose the Israelites to be examples to the world and to teach them His principles (Exodus 19:6, Isaiah 56:7). Therefore when the fullness of time came, God liberated His people from slavery in Egypt. He selected a leader from amongst them, Moses, who would lead them to freedom. Once they were physically liberated from bondage, God had to rebuild His image in their minds; to do so would require Him to also liberate their minds from slavery.

God could no longer rely on word of mouth to be the main mechanism to teach His principles of stewardship. While in slavery in Egypt, the children of Israel became isolated from God; they lost their desire and their ability to communicate with Him directly. They requested that Moses do the communicating with God on their behalf:

> Then they said to Moses, "You speak with us, and we
> will hear; but let not God speak with us, lest we die.
>
> Exodus 20:19

What a change in the attitude of the human race that once walked and talked with God; mankind now requested a mediator to go to God on our behalf. The Israelites became afraid of God and they lost respect for His principles. He had to define from scratch everything that they were required to do as His people; for example, He had to define how they should live as a people, settle disputes, etc.

Once the children of Israel left Egypt, God had to reestablish His image in their minds before they were allowed to enter Canaan – the Promised Land. God now moved to another phase in His plan of redemption for mankind. Since He would no longer depend solely on word of mouth, His principles and instructions were going to be written down. God began the process of documenting His principles and guidelines by writing on tables of stone - His Ten Commandments Law (Exodus 20). He summoned Moses to Mount Sinai and there He wrote the Ten Commandments. All of the principles and guidelines for stewardship are based on the Ten Commandments. When God wrote the Ten Commandments on the two tablets of stone, He was symbolizing their permanency and infallibility.

Moses wrote all the other dictations from God; thus began the Bible, the written word of God. God continued to dictate to Moses principles concerning civil practices as well as the specifications for His temple. The temple of God was to be a reminder to the children of Israel of His presence amongst them. Today, God no longer lives in man-made temples, but He lives in the temples of our hearts.

Having documented His principles and guidelines for stewardship, God ensured that they would be passed on through ages, from generation to generation, and down to you and me.

God demonstrated His love for the Israelites by freeing them from Egypt; now He was going to reveal to them His love for the entire human race. God rose from amongst them one, Moses, who led them to freedom from physical bondage. Using the principles of stewardship, He next demonstrated to them that once again from amongst them He would send One, Christ the Savior, who would liberate the entire world from the bondage of sin.

Just as God provided to the children of Israel principles for physical cleanliness (Exodus 19), He also provided them with principles for spiritual cleanliness – the Levitical (Leviticus 1- 5) system of offerings. A review of the Levitical system of offerings reveals to us the principles of stewardship. It was the same technique God used to teach the Israelites (Psalm 103:7).

The principles defined by God in the Levitical system of offerings form the building blocks on which true stewardship is built. If we are to understand the true spirituality of stewardship, we must first understand the principles as defined by God in the Levitical system of offerings.

If worshippers do not understand the key spiritual principles of stewardship, then it would be impossible for them to understand why they are required to be faithful stewards. We are called God's spiritual children of Israel. The Levitical system of offerings also holds for us important details of God's process of justification and redemption. These details are as relevant for us today as they were back then for the children of Israel.

The Significance of the Levitical Offerings Revealed

The purpose of this study is to understand the principles of stewardship contained in the Levitical system of offerings as defined by God.

God reestablished His Ten Commandments and then provided specific instructions for the erection of the temple in their midst. God first wrote and delivered the Ten Commandments to the Israelites because:

- They establish Him as the Creator of the world. The children of Israel watched as the Egyptian people created their gods from precious metals and stones; the true God was the creator of all the people and the precious metals and stones.
- They establish Him as the owner of everything and as the provider for His people. During their time in Egypt, the Israelites witnessed the Egyptians providing for their gods. They had to learn that the true God is omniscient, omnipresent, and omnipotent.
- They reestablished the authority and preeminence

of God.
- They establish the standards used to determine whether or not a sin was committed (1 John 3:4). After their Egyptian experience, the Israelites' ability to determine what was sin against God had become severely hampered. His commandments still serve the same purposes today as they did for the children of Israel back then; they are now written on the tables of our hearts (2 Corinthians 3:2).

The name used for God when He wrote the Ten Commandments was *Elohim*[2]. The name *Elohim* means that God is greater than all gods (Psalm 97:9), and it also helped the Israelites recognize that these other gods were false gods (Psalm 96:5; Isaiah 40:25; Isaiah 46:4).

Once His law was established and the reconstructive process had begun in the minds of the Israelites, God then provided specific instructions to Moses for the erection of the temple in their midst. The temple symbolized the presence of God amongst them.

The sequence of events in this period of their history is important. God first established His ownership of everything and then His authority in their lives. These are two (2) critical first steps in the life of a faithful steward. Once we allow the Holy Spirit to get that sequence of events complete in our lives, God can move us to the next step. He sets up camp with us; our bodies become His temple (1 Corinthian 3:16).

God used the Levitical system of offerings to teach the Israelites important aspects of His character, which were forgotten during their enslavement in Egypt. It was God's instructional material for them. Today we stand to benefit from those same lessons, if we are to follow God's principles of stewardship. How can anyone serve a God that he or she does not know (Leviticus 1:1,2)?

Once again, God instructed Moses to communicate to the Israelites that He was now ready to reveal to them His system of stewardship; it contained the details of His plan of salvation for the entire world. This is the plan of salvation that was designed before the foundation of the world, even before Adam and Eve had sinned.

God defined in excruciating details the principles of stewardship. Whenever God spends the time to identify the details of His principles, it is because the details contain enormous spiritual significance and meaning for the target audience.

There were five (5) principal offerings in the tabernacle, and these were given to Moses from the erected tabernacle at the foot of Mount Sinai. Before we begin our prayerful analysis of the Levitical system of offerings to extract the principles of stewardship, a few things are worth noting:

The Sacrifices – The Korbanot

In Chapter One, we defined the meaning of the Hebrew word Korban (plural – Korbanot) as symbolizing the individual's desire to come closer to God and to seek a relationship with Him. Every individual, including the priest, was required to bring a sacrifice to the altar. The act of offering a sacrifice to God was looked upon as favorable by Him and resulted in the individual receiving forgiveness for his or her sins.

We are all born in sin (Romans 3:23); therefore, we all must demonstrate our desire to come into a relationship with God – to come close to Him. When we allow God to use our talents, time, resources, influence, and abilities to do His will, we are symbolically bringing our sacrifice to the altar. Such acts constitute the practice of stewardship in our lives.

Sacrifices and the Name of God

Before God revealed the crucial concepts of His plan of salvation to the Israelites, He first revealed His principles and His character to them. These were key in reestablishing the image of God in their minds.

In biblical times, an individual's name was the revelation of his or her character. When a person's character changed in the Bible, his or her name also changed. For example Abram's name was changed to Abraham (Genesis 17:5), and Saul's name was changed to Paul (Acts 13:9). The Bible has many names for God, and they are windows through which His character is revealed to His people. The names of God reveal to us many important things about Him. What is so significant and amazing is how God uses names to reveal Himself and His plan for us, to us.

The name of God exclusively used in regard to korbanot (the sacrifices) is not "El" nor Elohim (but) rather YHVH (This is four Hebrew letters (Yod, He, Waw and He) called the "Tetragrammaton" – the English transliteration is 'Yahweh') the unique name, (so) that no one should think that the korban (sacrifice) is in order to feed God. The name YHVH refers to the transcendent aspect of God; it is the name, which indicates that God is beyond man's understanding.

The name Elohim, on the other hand, refers to God as judge, a concept that humans can grasp. Had this name of God been used in connection with offerings, one might have been tempted to imagine that a "bribe" is possible. But when we contemplate that the offerings are commanded by YHVH, we realize that no bribes can be offered. Additionally, YHVH – the singular, timeless name – refers to God's trait of existing outside of time.

This may help us understand how forgiveness takes place: If a man sinned yesterday, and repented today, how can his present attitude undo that which he did yesterday? If we understand that God exists outside of time – indeed, God created time – when we try to reestablish a relationship with God, then time becomes less of a factor. When man connects with the transcendent God, "yesterday" becomes limited to the human perspective, which no longer confines him.[3]

Repentance, Return and Forgiveness

> This is the mystery of "teshuva", repentance (which literally means "return") and of forgiveness. Man repents, returns to God, and God forgives him. This also explains why the word "korban" is derived from the root k-r-v, "to come close." The "korban" is the act which allows man to come close to God. "Teshuva" is not only a return to God, it is also a return to oneself, to the potential within man, to the image of God within each and every one of us.
>
> When man repents, he returns to the core of godliness within himself, that "tzelem Elohim," the "image of God" that is his essence. The importance of the "korban" lies in the rehabilitation of man, which is its intended result. The key is in man's rehabilitation, in his finding the image of God within him.[4]

The Reason for the Levitical System of Offerings

> The offerings were intended as a means toward an end, a path toward finding one's own "tzelem Elohim." They were meant to be the key which would allow faltering man to regain focus and not some sort of magical ritual needed to placate an angry God.[5]

The Levitical system of offerings was given by God to help man understand His plan of redemption for the world. The offerings or sacrifices pointed to the coming of the Messiah.

The Levitical system of offerings revealed God's principles of stewardship. His plan of salvation and redemption for the human race is veiled in the principles of stewardship.

When Christ came and died on Mount Calvary, the Levitical system of offerings was fulfilled in Him. It does not mean that it no longer holds any spiritual significance; as a matter of fact, it contains equally important lessons for us today as we look forward to the second coming of Christ, for we are now spiritual Israelites (Galatians 3:29; 6:16; 1 Corinthians12: 13; Romans 2:17, 25, 26, 28, 29).

First Principle Offering: The Burnt Offering

The *olah*[6] is the Hebrew name for burnt offering (Leviticus 1:3) and it means to "go up to". This sacrifice was the only sacrifice that was completely burnt in the fire on the altar. The offering was to be a male without blemish and it foreshadows the total sacrifice of Christ on the Cross of Calvary. This offering was required of all of Israel regularly every morning and evening (Exodus 29:38-42) and on Sabbath double that of the daily offering (Numbers 28:9). This offering signified the individual consecrating himself or herself to Yahweh. The offering was to be made of the individual's own free will.

> The offering was according to possession, which it was thought denoted a man's standing in society and before God. If the social standing of the offerer (worshipper) was such that he owned a herd then he should offer a bullock. A lamb was not acceptable to God from him. If, however, the offerer did not own a herd but did have a flock, then his offering must be a sheep or a goat. If neither a herd or a flock were owned, then the offering should be a bird (turtledoves or pigeons).[7]

God did not require the individual to bring to the altar a gift that was unaffordable. If He did, the individual could have been tempted to steal in an attempt to acquire that which he did not possess; God does not tempt us. The individual who could afford it brought a more expensive sacrifice to the altar. Jesus said to Scribes and Pharisees, *"For everyone to whom much is given, from him much will be required"* (Luke 12:48).

God simply requested the Israelites to offer to Him the best of what they possessed (2 Corinthians 9:7). One of the principles of true stewardship is that we must reserve our best for God. If you have great influence, you are to subject that to the will and direction of God. If you are a good teacher, then spend time teaching and explaining to others God's word. Whatever God has given to you, use it willingly to benefit others. Do not trivialize your gift(s) by comparing it to that of another, but simply focus on using every opportunity to use that gift(s) for a worthy and moral cause.

In Leviticus 1:4, we discover that the worshippers laid their hands upon the sacrifice, which symbolized that they had transferred their sins to the animal; the individual no longer had the sin. Justification had occurred at the time of the sacrifice of the animal on the altar. The individual, not a substitute, then killed the innocent animal with a knife (signifying the future death of Jesus on the cross). After killing the animal, the sin is symbolically in the animal's blood. The priest took blood from the animal, thus transferring the individual' sin to the priest. The animal's blood symbolized the atoning blood of Christ. The priest then sprinkled the blood all around the altar. The individual's sin was now transferred to the altar.

Leviticus 1 verse 6 has the offerer skinning and cutting it [the animal] into pieces. The skin was the only part of the animal that wasn't burnt, the skin being a memorial of the death of the sacrifice. The skin provided him with a covering, a robe of righteousness, reminding us that God had to kill an animal to clothe Adam and Eve with its skin covering their embarrassment.

The priests kept the skin as their portion, the offerer left not with the physical covering but with the spiritual covering and the sense that God had provided everything. We see Christ's sacrifice as clothing us with righteousness and that He takes away our embarrassment (guilt) as we enter Gods presence to worship Him.

In Leviticus 1 verses 7-9 the priests prepared the

altar and placed on it the head and the fat [of the animal offering]. The offerer washes the inner parts and the legs with water before the priests placed the pieces on the altar so that it was all burnt.

The inspection meant there was no outward blemish; the washing showed there was no inward blemish. Man and God scrutinized Christ both outwardly and inwardly respectively. Man could find no fault in Him and God could see no fault in Him.[8]

The Fire – God was in the fire (Hebrews 12:29). He purifies our sacrifices allowing them to rise before Him as a sweet aroma.

The Head – represents the mind and the intellect. *Let this mind be in you which was also in Christ Jesus* (Philippians 2:5).

The Inwards – represents the will and the emotions. If we allow the Holy Spirit to, He will bring our will and emotions under His control (Galatians 5:22,23).

The Legs – We must walk in the paths of righteousness (Psalm 23).

The Fat – represents the best part of the animal. It meant that the animal was healthy. The fat was to be burnt on the altar, signifying that our best is for God. The acceptance of the offering by God signified to the individual that God had accepted him or her as righteous. His or her righteousness was imputed. The worshipper had achieved closeness to God.

Key Principles of Stewardship From the Burnt Offering

(a) Anyone was allowed to bring a burnt offering. God is an inclusive God, male or female; everyone is required to be a faithful steward.

(b) The burnt offering was a male without blemish, the best of the individual's flock. It would have been prime breeding stock, of great personal value to the worshipper. To offer it on the altar was a significant personal sacrifice on the part of the individual. God requires the best from us and not some from the rest; this symbolizes that we are offering Him our all. It also signifies that it is truly sacrificial giving.

(c) The burnt offering symbolized the death of Christ on the cross (Hebrews 13:10). It was to be done regularly and every time the individual brought the burnt offering as their sacrifice, it served as a reminder that one day the promised Messiah would shed His blood for the remissions of their sins.

(d) The fat signified the best parts of the animal were reserved for God. The expression "fat" is often used in figurative senses, e.g. abundant, exuberant, lusty, fertile, robust, and outwardly successful (Luke 15: 22-24; Psalms 119:70; Proverbs 11:25; 13:4). Once again God emphasizes that we are to reserve our best for Him. Whenever God repeats a principle, it is to communicate its importance to us.

(e) A portion of the offering, the skin, was for the priest. God expects us to give of our finances and resources to support the people who dedicate their lives to working in ministry for Him.

(f) The consumption of the offering signified that the individual had been justified by their faith. Stewardship is a prerequisite for salvation.

(g) The offering signified to the Israelites that they were in a covenant relationship with a God who loved them. It allowed them to demonstrate their love to God. God demonstrated His love for us by giving His Son to die on Calvary for us (John 3:16). When we faithfully follow the principles of stewardship, we demonstrate our love for God (John 14:15).

(h) The individual made the offering to God of his or her own free will. While stewardship is a requirement from God to us, we must fulfill that requirement willingly. If we grudgingly perform acts of stewardship, due to peer pressure or for any other reasons, God does not accept such acts as compliant with His request. In His sight, it is as if we are unfaithful stewards.

Stewardship must be an integral part of our lives. The act of giving of our possessions should not be relegated to some seasonal event (Christmas or Easter) but must occur daily. The decisions we make daily to be the best for Christ strengthens our resolve to become faithful stewards.

Second Principle Offering:
The Grain or Meal Offering

The *minhah*[8] is the Hebrew name for grain or meal offering. While the wealthier individual could bring a cattle, a less wealthy person would bring a sheep, and an even less fortunate individual would bring a turtledove. For the least fortunate individual who wanted to offer something, they could offer a meal or grain offering (Leviticus 2). With the variety of offerings, God allowed everyone, regardless of his or her social or financial status, the opportunity to offer a sacrifice before Him. God gave everyone the opportunity to participate.

The grain or meal offering was offered in relation to the blood offerings and usually followed the burnt offering. This offering signified the giving of thanks to Yahweh by the Israelites for provision of their daily needs and for forgiveness of their sins.

The meal offerings were brought to one of the priests, who then took it to the altar and cast a "memorial portion" on the fire. He did this also with the incense. A "memorial portion" of a grain offering was a small portion burnt on the altar in place of the whole amount. The rest of the offering was a gift to the priest to support his ministry, unless he was bringing the meal offering for himself where he would burn the whole thing. The Hebrew word for memorial portion, *azkarah*[9], is related to the Hebrew verb for remember, **zakar**. It signified that the worshipper remembered God's graciousness and generosity in bestowing His blessings on him or her. The grain or meal offering was something pleasant and sweet to God, with no thought of sin bearing or cleansing of sin in the offering. The grain offering had some powerful references to God's presence amongst His people.

The meal offerings were either public or private and were either brought with a burnt or peace offering or alone, but they were never brought with a sin or trespass offering. The grain or meal offering had four major ingredients, each of which had spiritual meaning and significance. The sacrifices burnt on the altar are called the "bread of God" which signified Christ. *For the bread of God is He who comes down from heaven and gives life to the world* (John 6:33). Jesus is the "bread of life" (John 6:48). The burnt meal offerings symbolized to the Israelites the coming of the promised Messiah who would shed His blood for the remissions of their sins.

There were four (4) types of grain or meal offerings that were associated with circumstances or property of the individual.

The uncooked flour – Leviticus 2:1

Bread baked in an oven – Leviticus 2:4

Bread prepared on a griddle – Leviticus 2:5

Bread cooked in a pan – Leviticus 2:7

In presenting the offering the offerer (worshipper) simply came to the door of the tabernacle having prepared it as instructed and gave it to the priests. There was no ceremony just simple submission, for there was nothing meritorious in his action only obedience.

The priest received the meal offering from him, took a handful of the grain or cakes, with all the frankincense and burned it on the altar. The remainder belonged to the priests.

Aaron and his sons in the court of the tabernacle ate it. Only a small portion of this offering belonged to God, but it was a memorial, which means that the handful represented the whole in the sight of God and was accepted by Him as the whole.[10]

Fine Flour

The fine flour was made from the best grain of wheat. The millstones ground the wheat as fine as possible, and then it was finely sifted to remove any coarseness, unevenness, and empty husks. This flour was fit for the king's table. It was the basis of the "bread of life". Like blood was to the animal, the fine flour was to the bread. Christ's life was perfect and His accusers declared that they had "found no fault in Him" (Luke 23:4). Wheat is also used in the Bible to represent the true believer (Matthew 3:12; 13). In order to perfect our character, our lives must go through the millstones of trials and temptations so that Christ could remove our coarseness, our unevenness and our empty husks.

Oil

The oil was poured upon the flour, it is spoken of as being 'anointed' with oil in Leviticus 7:12. Oil is of course a symbol of the Holy Spirit. If the fine flour is seen as Christ's perfect life anointed with the oil of the Holy Spirit, we clearly see the symbolism of the Messiah being the anointed one visible in the offering.

The anointing is also for the believer, yet it is necessary for the preparation of the millstone's grinding. There was oil on and oil in the cakes (verse 5,6). The anointing was to do with the outward working of the Holy Spirit, while the mingling speaks of the inward working of the Holy Spirit, the indwelling. Just as every part of Christ's life, every thought, every word, every deed, was mingled (saturated) with the Holy Spirit, so should ours.[11]

Frankincense

The frankincense symbolized the divinity of God. It was very costly incense that was not native to Israel, but its fragrance and value enhanced the grain offering. It allowed the offering when burnt on the altar to be a sweet savor to God. It was the fire that drew the fragrance. When we come under trials, it is the time when we should be at our best for Christ. As faithful stewards, we must also manage our tempers and tongues and bring them under the control of God.

Salt

Another important ingredient was salt, which was to be added to every sacrifice. Salt is best known for its purifying (prevents corruption) and preserving properties. The Israelites had no Maytag refrigerators, so they used salt to preserve and purify their food. Both of these properties are relevant in biblical references to salt.

> Christ's influence purified the lives of those He came into contact with; believers are called to be the salt of the earth (Matthew 5:13). Salt is the emblem of incorruption and Christ's body saw no corruption (Psalm 16:10). Salt is also the emblem of divine grace (Colossians 4:6) and Christ's words are always health giving and wholesome.[12]

Finally, it is called "the salt of the covenant" in Leviticus 2:13. This refers to the preserving properties of salt. Every offering that contained salt was to remind the individual of the covenant God made with Israel at Mount Sinai and of his or her obligation and privilege to remain faithful to God; salt was seen as the seal of friendship. When we follow the principles of stewardship, God wants us to remember that we are in an everlasting covenant relationship with Him.

There were two substances that were forbidden from use in the offering (verse 11), leaven and honey. Whereas salt was an emblem of incorruption, leaven is the emblem of corruption (of hypocrisy – Luke 12:1; of pride – 1 Corinthians 5:6; of sin – 1 Corinthians 5:7,8; of false teaching – Galatians 5:9; of self-indulgence – Mark 8:1). To mix the holy things of God (salt) with unholy things of the world (leaven) is an abomination unto the Lord (Hophi and Phinehas, 1 Samuel 2:12).

Honey represents things that are sweet and pleasing and attractive to the flesh and to the natural man. When honey is burnt, it begins to ferment and turns sour; the smell of burning honey is very different from the fragrance of burning incense.

Key Principles of Stewardship From the Grain/ Meal Offering

In addition to reinforcing the principles revealed in the burnt offering, since this may have been to a different clientele (less wealthy), the grain or meal offering provided some additional stewardship principles.

(a) The salt signified the individual was in a covenant relationship with God. Stewardship was designed by God to provide a mechanism for man to reconnect with God.

(b) The fact that no leaven or honey was added to the offering signified the holiness of the offering to God. The principles of stewardship are holy and should not be defiled by us.

(c) The grain or meal offering was a thank offering to God. This was a special offering following some success the individual experienced, for example a very bountiful grain harvest. As a part of our adherence to the principles of stewardship, it is a biblically recommended practice to include a thank offering to God when special events occur in our lives. Such events could include, but should not be limited to, job promotions, graduation, birth of a baby, new home or car, marriage or milestone anniversary, and answer to a special prayer. Anything for which you feel especially grateful to God should be celebrated with a thank offering to Him.

Final Thoughts

An analysis of the Levitical system of offerings yields a deeper understanding and appreciation of God's plan of salvation; it contained the blue print for salvation. It also reveals the principles of stewardship that we are to follow as we strive to become faithful stewards.

The Levitical system of offerings was full of rituals. There was no material available to read and learn of God; they learned through repeatedly performing the rituals of the Levitical system of offerings. Whenever Levitical offerings were presented, bystanders gathered in the outer court to watch the events thereby learning from them. Just as bystanders learned by watching others present their offerings, by being a faithful steward we can also help others to become better stewards, either by their observance of our practices or by them benefiting from our benevolence.

The principles of stewardship revealed by the study of the burnt offering and the grain and meal offering can be summarized as follows:

(a) **We must have an intimate relationship with God if we are to be faithful stewards;** otherwise, the principles of stewardship become a set of burdensome rules. God is supreme (Elohim) in our lives.

(b) **Stewardship is a personal matter between the individual and God.**

(c) **God is the owner of everything; He gave us everything we possess (Yahweh).**

(d) **God requires everyone to be a faithful steward of his or her time, talent, possessions, and influence.**

(e) **God requires those who have been blessed with more to give more (Luke 12:48).** This does not mean or imply that there are different levels of stewardship. However there are two (2) types of stewards: a faithful steward and an unfaithful steward.

(f) **God requires the best from us.** Our gifts must mean something to us; they must be motivated by our love for God and originate from our hearts. That's why God respects sacrificial giving and not superficial giving.

(g) **The principles of stewardship find deeper meaning in our lives when we relate them to Christ's sacrifice on Calvary.**

(h) **God requires us to give of our finances and resources to support the people who dedicate their lives to working in ministry for Him.**

(i) **Stewardship is a prerequisite for salvation.** The act of giving of our possessions should not be tied to seasonal events (Christmas or Easter). We strive daily towards achieving it.

(j) **When God returns, He will confer on us one of two rewards: faithful steward or unfaithful steward.**

(k) **Following the principles of stewardship allows us to demonstrate our love for God (John 14:15).**

(l) **Our commitment to stewardship must be voluntary.**

The exposition of the principles of stewardship from the remaining principle offerings in the Levitical system of offerings continues in the next chapter.

References:

1. Hebrew #6754 – *Strong's Dictionary of Hebrew and Greek Words*
2. Hebrew #430 – *Strong's Dictionary of Hebrew and Greek Words*
3. *"Genesis – In the beginning, Gen.1:1-5:8"* – Messianic Rabbi Tom Barnes
4. *"The Mystery of the Sacrifices (Leviticus 1-5)"* – Rabbi Moshe ben Nachman
5. Ibid
6. Hebrew #5930 – *Strong's Dictionary of Hebrew and Greek Words.*
7. *"The Mystery of the Sacrifices (Leviticus 1-5)"* – Rabbi Moshe ben Nachman
8. Hebrew #4503 - *Strong's Dictionary of Hebrew and Greek Words*
9. Hebrew #234 - *Strong's Dictionary of Hebrew and Greek Words*
10. *The Village Pastor's Simple Guide to the Offerings of the Tabernacle,* compiled from material in the following books:
    • *Dictionary of the Bible* by Grant & Rowley
    • *Expository Dictionary* by W.E. Vine
    • *Daily Bible Study* by William Barclay
    • *Expositors Bible Commentary* by   Frank E.

Gaebelein
- *Ungers Bible Dictionary* by Merrill F. Unger
- *Wycliffe Bible Encyclopedia* by C.F. Pfeiffer, H.F. Vos and J. Rea
- *Thus Shalt Thou Serve* by C. W. Slemming
- *These Are the Garments* by C. W. Slemming
- *Made According to Pattern* by C. W. Slemming
- *Hastings Bible Dictionary* by James Hastings
- *God's Tabernacle in the Wilderness* by John Carter

11. Ibid
12. Ibid

*And as it is appointed for men to die once, but after
this the judgment, so Christ was offered once to
bear the sins of many. To those who eagerly wait
for Him He will appear a second time,
apart from sin, for salvation.*

Hebrews 9:27,28

5

The Levitical System of Offerings:
The Principles of Stewardship Revealed
Part 2

❖⋅═◯═⋅❖

As we continue our analysis of the Levitical system of offerings, we must pause to appreciate the order in which these
offerings were presented because of its spiritual significance.

When God gave the specifications to Moses for the tabernacle
and its furnishings, He began with the mercy seat and worked
outward from there. This signified God reaching out to man in
grace. However, man's approach to God is in the opposite order. We
find this same trend with the offerings. God began with the burnt
offering and ended with the trespass offering; man's approach to
God began at the trespass offering and culminated with the burnt
offering, since we have to first deal with the sins in our individual
lives before we can have a relationship with God.

After we have sought and received forgiveness of our sins from
God, we come to a place of increased consecration to the Lord; we

enjoy sweet fellowship with Him. The individual being allowed to eat of the peace offering signified this fellowship with God. We must first establish a relationship with God, meaning our lives revolve around Him, before we can begin the path to becoming a faithful steward. Consider the **Stewardship Equation:**

Relationship With God + Adherence to the Principles of Stewardship = A Faithful Steward

Establishing a relationship with God is an ongoing daily activity for as long as we live (Romans 6:13, 1 Corinthians 15:31). Therefore achieving the status of a "faithful steward" is an ongoing daily process, which culminates with the return of Christ. If we allow the Holy Spirit to achieve the first two (2) factors of the **Stewardship Equation** in our lives, when Christ, the Master, returns He will confer upon us the reward of *"well done good and faithful servant [steward]"* (Matthew 25:23).

The analysis of the first two offerings in the Levitical system of offerings, burnt offering and the grain or meal offering, revealed several key principles of stewardship. God used each of the offerings in the system to teach very specific aspects of His plan of salvation. He also used them to reinforce common themes. Since the analysis thus far has extracted several of the principles of stewardship, we shall do a more concise analysis of the remaining offerings in an attempt to reveal any additional principles.

Third Principle Offering: The Sin Offering

The *chataat*[1] is the Hebrew name for sin offering. This offering was required to be offered by every Israelite. The purpose of this offering was to make atonement for the individual who committed unintentional sins. This type of sin applied only to sins committed through ignorance, as opposed to those committed presumptuously.

Unintentional sins were not only committed through lack of knowledge but also were those that were not premeditated, or those committed through weakness, or where the offender at the time did not realize his or her guilt; such sins come from the weakness of our human nature rather than a determined, presumptuous defiant rebellion against God and His commands.

Sin is repulsive to God and it separates us from Him and breaks our fellowship with Him. He is a holy God and sin cannot exist in His presence. The objective of the sin offering was for the repentant individual to obtain forgiveness for his or her sins (Leviticus 4:20, 26, 31, 35) and to obtain cleansing from the pollution of those sins (Leviticus 12:8, 14:20, 16:19).

> The animals to be sacrificed varied to the position or status of the sinner. The priests as well as the whole congregation were required to offer a bullock. The leader or ruler offered a male goat while a member of the community offered a female goat or lamb.
>
> In each case the sacrifice had to be perfect, that is without defect or blemish.[2]

The phrase "unintentionally" sin (Leviticus 4:1, 13, 22, 27) is repeated with the clear assertion of guilt, so that the responsibility is not easily pushed aside. Even when unaware, that state of unawareness does not provide us with an excuse for falling short of God's commands. Since our adherence to the principles of stewardship draws us closer to God, it heightens our awareness of sin in our lives. As a result of our heightened awareness of sin, we find ourselves more readily seeking God's forgiveness and His protection from committing unintentional sins.

> Three times in Leviticus 4 verses 14, 23, 28, the Bible states, "When they become aware or when he is made aware" the purpose of the law was to make the people aware of their unintentional sins so that they would not repeat them and so that they could be forgiven. The offerer would bring the sacrifice to the gate of the tabernacle, the place designated by God.

God did not allow this sacrifice for sin to be made just anywhere. This would have led to uncontrolled practices eventually leading to idolatry.

The offerer was to lay his hands upon the head of the animal to be sacrificed; in the case of the whole congregation it was done by the elders as representatives of the community. This act had a two-fold significance; the first was identification and the second was imputation. They identified themselves with the animal that was about to die. Because of their faith they believed that when they laid their hands on the animal sacrifice, their sins were transferred from them to the animal.[3]

The individuals came to the altar bearing the guilt of their sins, but they left the altar having atoned for their sins; righteousness was at that moment imparted to them. In the sight of the almighty God, they left the altar as if they had not sinned.

When we confess our sins before God and we believe in Him and accept Him as Lord of our lives, it is as if we did not sin. As we earnestly follow the principles of stewardship, the Holy Spirit reinforces in our subconscious mind that God is able to forgive us of our sins and cleanse us from our guilt (1 John 1:9). Stewardship was designed by God to be an integral part of the daily process of sanctification in our lives.

When we fail to follow God's principles of true stewardship, we miss the reminders and markers He has placed along the way. We become despondent over our predisposition to sin, and we find ourselves becoming separated from the One who could save us. Failure to follow the principles of stewardship creates an opportunity for sin to become more prevalent in our lives. The reason is quite simple. When an individual is not striving to be a faithful steward, he or she is stealing from God. Once an individual begins to steal from God, it becomes easier to steal from others; it becomes easier to lie and to cheat. Sinfulness leads to more sinfulness.

True stewardship is not about money or about what we have or what we can do. It is a holy system from God designed for the believer of God.

Key Principles of Stewardship From the Sin Offering

The analysis of the sin offering shows that it reinforces the principles of stewardship and the elements of God's plan of salvation revealed in the burnt and meal or grain offerings.

Fourth Principle Offering:
The Trespass Offering

The *asham*[4] is the Hebrew word for the trespass offering. The sin offering (chattaah) and trespass offering (ashaam) appear to be very similar, but prayerful analysis reveals the following:

The sin offering was designed by God to help the Israelites comprehend the problem of the sinful nature of man; this sinful nature was inherited from Adam. On the other hand, the trespass offering was designed by God to help the Israelites comprehend the problem of the many actual sins they committed.

Our sinful acts or acts of sin are a direct result of our sinful nature. After Adam sinned, it is as if we became genetically altered to sin (Romans 5:12), and without Christ in our lives, all our acts are sinful (Isaiah 64:6).

The trespass offering allowed God to reveal to the Israelites that their many actual sins committed not only offended God, but they also offended and hurt their fellow men. Every time a person cheats, lies, slanders or attacks, these acts of sin often bring harm and suffering to others.

This offering allows us to understand the sacrificial death of Christ from another angle. He not only died for our sinful nature, but He also died for the many acts of sin we have committed and will commit against God and men.

This offering consisted of a ram without blemish, which was valued by the priest according to the sanctuary shekel. The ram was slain on the northern side of the altar and its blood was sprinkled against the side of the altar with the remainder being poured out at the base of the altar. The priest then burnt the fat of the animal on the bronze altar while he kept the rest of the animal as a gift. So as not to exclude anyone, if a person was unable to afford a ram, then the priest would accept two doves or pigeons, if that proved to be still unaffordable, then the priest accepted fine flour. If the individual brought fine flour, because it was a sin offering, no oil or frankincense was added to it. This was reminder that sin is distasteful to God and we can't make it a "sweet savor in His sight. Now the procedure was different depending on whether the trespass was against a man or God.

The order of things when the trespass was against God (failure to return tithes, offerings, etc):

1. SACRIFICE – substitution, atonement.
2. RESTITUTION – restoration for the wrong.
3. A FIFTH MORE – recompense added

Here the thought of the atoning sacrifice was predominant.

The order when the trespass was against a fellow man was:

1. RESTITUTION – restoration for the wrong.
2. RECOMPENSE – the fifth was added as compensation.
3. SACRIFICE – atonement for the sin.

The thought of restitution to the injured (affected) party was predominant. But mere restitution would not suffice; there must also be atonement for the sin against the Lord. Jesus re-enforced the law and the order of restitution. In Matthew 5:23, 24, it shows that restitution came first and then the altar (sacrifice). Our communion with God is broken until restitution is made; we must get it right with our fellow man first. Why not add a gift by way of compensation to the person?[5]

Key Principles of Stewardship From the Trespass Offering

God used the trespass offering to introduce the concept of restitution to the Israelites. This implied restoration for wrong doing by the one who committed the act.

This offering reveals an additional stewardship principle. God uses our gifts to bless others, therefore, when we fail to return our gifts to Him, in addition to robbing God (Malachi 3:10) we are also robbing someone the opportunity to experience His goodness. God does not have to use us to provide for the needs of others, but He gives us an opportunity to be a part of His loving kindness and mercy.

Fifth Principle Offering: The Peace or Fellowship Offering

The *shelem*[6] is the Hebrew word for the peace or fellowship offering. It was the third offering commanded by God, but in practice it took place last. This was significant, for only after the individual met the needs of his fellow man and the requirements of God could he experience and enjoy true peace and fellowship with God and his fellow man. The reason why some of us can't find peace in this troubled world or are having problems in our spiritual relationship with God is because we have neglected the principles of stewardship (Hebrews 12:14).

This offering expressed fellowship between the individual and God. It consisted of three (3) types: the Thank offering (the Hebrew word is *towdah*) that expressed gratitude for an unexpected blessing, the Votive offering (the Hebrew word is *neder*) that expressed thanks for a blessing granted when a vow or pledge had been made while asking for a blessing, and the Freewill offering (the Hebrew word is *nedabah*) that expressed thanks to God without regard to any specific blessing, just for Him being God. The peace offering was the only offering that the worshipper was able to partake of.

The rejoicing of God's people before Him and the blessedness of eating and drinking in the kingdom of God marked this time of fellowship.

Key Principles of Stewardship From the Peace Offering

The peace offering was special; God, the priests, and the worshipper shared it. It was the final offering in the sequence of offerings, and it symbolized that the individual had completed all the requirements for fellowship with God and his or her neighbor.

Once we adhere to the principles of stewardship, motivated by God's love, we find ourselves in a relationship with Him (symbolic of peace with Him). Our acts of stewardship benefit our neighbors, so we find ourselves at peace with them. The primitive human instincts of greed and guilt are eliminated from our lives.

Final Thoughts

The analysis of the five principal offerings in the Levitical system of offerings (Part 1 and Part 2) revealed God's principles of stewardship. Since we will be judged by these principles, we are required to live by them. When Christ returns, as King of Kings and Lord of Lords, He will confer on us one of two (2) titles: faithful steward or unfaithful steward. The extent to which we obey the principles of stewardship in our daily lives will determine which title is conferred on us. Only the faithful stewards will make it into the kingdom of heaven; those who proved trustworthy with God's property on earth will be allowed access to His property in heaven.

The sacrifices identified in these offerings all pointed to the death of Christ. The death of Christ on Mount Calvary abolished the need for the physical sacrifices (2 Corinthians 5:19, Romans 5:10,11) of the Levitical system of offerings. Christ's death was the fulfillment of the promises contained in the system of the physical sacrifices. God also used the Levitical system of offerings to teach the Israelites important spiritual lessons that remain valid for us today. One such lesson is salvation by grace through faith in Christ (Ephesians 2:8,9). The Israelites saw in the Levitical system of offerings a foretaste of salvation in the promised Messiah; we see in them the outline of the plan of salvation, which we now experience because of the death of the Messiah on the cross.

By neglecting to understand the Old Testament Levitical system of offerings, many Christians miss a deeper understanding of Christ's sacrifice on Calvary. We can't begin to relate to God's principles of true stewardship unless we take the time to read and understand the principles of the Levitical system of offerings.

References:

1. Hebrew #2403 - *Strong's Dictionary of Hebrew and Greek Words.*
2. *The Village Pastor's Simple Guide to the Offerings of the Tabernacle,* compiled from material in the following books:
   * *Dictionary of the Bible* by Grant & Rowley
   * *Expository Dictionary* by W.E. Vine
   * *Daily Bible Study* by William Barclay
   * *Expositors Bible Commentary* by Frank E. Gaebelein
   * *Ungers Bible Dictionary* by Merrill F. Unger
   * *Wycliffe Bible Encyclopedia* by C.F. Pfeiffer, H.F.Vos and J. Rea
   * *Thus Shalt Thou Serve* by C. W. Slemming
   * *These Are the Garments* by C. W. Slemming
   * *Made According to Pattern* by C. W. Slemming
   * *Hastings Bible Dictionary* by James Hastings
   * *God's Tabernacle in the Wilderness* by John Carter
3. Ibid.
4. Hebrew #817 - *Strong's Dictionary of Hebrew and Greek*

Words.

5. *The Village Pastor's Simple Guide to the Offerings of the Tabernacle.*

6. Hebrew #8002 - *Strong's Dictionary of Hebrew and Greek Words.*

"I have held many things in my hands and I have lost them all. But whatever I have placed in God's hands, that I still possess."

Martin Luther

6

Why Does God Want a Gift From Me?

During the analysis of the Levitical system of offerings, we discovered that God first established Himself as the sovereign One (the owner) in the Israelites' minds. Once that was accomplished, He proceeded to define for them the series of sacrifices they were required to bring to the altar. If we are to be faithful stewards, we must first establish the sovereignty and ownership of God in our minds. If we fail to accomplish that critical first step, we experience great difficulty in understanding and willingly following the principles of stewardship in our lives.

> Too often we either lose the focus or forget our position. It is the devil's plan to blind our eyes to the ownership of God [so] that he can have us believe that what we manage is really ours. It is when we are thus blinded that our hearts become lifted up with pride, believing that we have so much, and sometimes "having need of nothing." The danger inherent in such feelings is that there is the tendency to be less dependent on God.[1]

Knowing God's character is crucial to being a faithful steward of His property. When an individual has a wrong concept of God in his or her mind, he or she incorrectly believes that God is a begrudging giver and a harsh taskmaster, rather than a benevolent and loving God.

Once the Israelites became aware of God's authority and ownership, He was then able to begin the process of moving them to the next phase in the reconstruction of His image in their minds. Once they recognized and accepted the sovereignty of God, they were mentally and spiritually prepared to willingly bring their offerings to the altar.

God created us (Colossians 1:16), and because of Adam and Eve's sin Satan laid claim to us; Christ bought us back with His precious blood (1 Corinthians 6:19-20, 1 Peter 1:18,19). God anointed Him as Lord of everything. (Ephesians 1:20-23; Acts 10:36; Romans 10:12); that authenticated God as the owner of everything - our life, our very existence, our personality, our influence, our success. Everything we possess belongs to Him. The question we should be asking ourselves is, "why wouldn't I want to give a gift to God who owns everything?"

> Once we allow the Holy Spirit to establish in our
> minds Christ as Lord of our lives, we can willingly
> and without grudge return to Him a portion of what
> He has given to us; then our motives become pure
> and we begin to see ourselves in a covenant relation-
> ship with Him.

You have heard this question asked concerning someone who is perceived to have a lot, "what do you give to the person who has everything?" The answer is nothing but love! God is not interested in our gifts or sacrifices. He is interested in the message that we send to Him and to the world when we willingly follow the principles of stewardship. When we follow the principles of stewardship, we communicate the following messages to God and to the onlookers in the world:

- God, we love you.
- Because we love you, God, we reserve our best for you (I Corinthians 16:2).
- God, we recognize you as the owner of everything.
- God, we recognize you as our provider.
- God, we recognize that we are in a covenant relationship with you. Our regular and systematic giving is an indication that the covenant relationship is alive in our lives.
- God, we desire to come close to you (Ephesians 2:13).
- We believe in and accept the death of Christ on the cross as our sacrifice.
- Since He came the first time, we believe that He will come again to receive us into heaven (Acts 1:11).

Our sacrifice is anything that God requires of us to accomplish His will in our lives; it includes but is not limited to, our possessions, our time, our talents, our influence, and our abilities.

When we willingly bring our gifts to the altar, a portion of our gift is reserved by God to be used to sustain His priest and to cover the expenses incurred in the promulgation of His work (Mark 6:7, Luke 8:1-3, 1 Corinthians 9:13,14, 1 Corinthians 16:1-2, 2 Corinthians 11:9, Galatians 6:10, Philippians 4:10-18, 3 John 1:5 - 8). By allowing the priest to keep a portion of the offerings in the Levitical system of offerings, God sanctioned this practice.

The expenses incurred in spreading God's work include such things as the upkeep of the church building, the hymn books, the lesson guides and all such items used in the furtherance of His knowledge to the members of the congregation or the community – both local or worldwide. It is the Christian's duty to give financial support to the gospel. Any member who goes to church but gives nothing or does nothing to support the work of the Lord is derelict in his or her duties to God. God views such an individual in the same manner as He (the Master) viewed the servant who buried his talent (Matthew 25:14-28).

Throughout the Bible we read that God created everything and everyone (Psalm 51:16; James 1:17), so it would be reasonable and logical to conclude that He does not need anything from us. Why then would He implement the plan of stewardship, which requires the creature to bring an offering or gift to the Creator? It would be as if we, as parents, requested our children to return to us a portion of the allowance that we gave to them.

At first glance that may seem absurd, but consider this, we do encourage our children to put aside a portion of their allowance for savings. The portion that they decide to save is returned to us and we open a savings account in the bank for them. We don't need the money from them, and we could have just withheld the savings amount in the first place. However, we use this process as a mechanism to teach our children important lessons about making decisions on savings and investments later on in life. Likewise our heavenly Father doesn't need any gifts or offerings from us, His children, but He uses the principles of stewardship to teach us important lessons about salvation and successful living. He could have withheld His portion and given to us that what He deemed necessary. Since we are in a covenant relationship with Him, He gave us everything and He trusts us to be faithful in returning His portion; He wants us to succeed as faithful stewards.

The answer to the question "Why does God want a gift from me?" could simply be, "because He said so in His word"(1 Corinthians 16:1,2; 1 Timothy 6:17-19), but that would be the wrong reason to obey. God did not make us like robots; He made us of a sound mind (2 Timothy 1:7) and He gave us the ability to choose. Therefore, the answer to the above question is driven by our love for God and our spiritual connection with Him. Since God has given us everything, including His Son who came to earth to die for us, we should feel privileged and excited that He has also given us an opportunity to give something back to Him. God expects us to give what we are capable of giving (2 Corinthians 8:12). The subject of giving is mentioned more often in the Bible than love or praying; it is mentioned 2,162 times. There are more promises related to giving than any other subject. How can our love for God be real unless it is expressed in our obedience and our giving?

Our reason for observing God's principles of stewardship must be voluntary and based on pure motives driven by our love for God (Matthew 5:8). God will not accept our gifts if they are based on coercion or if our motives are not out of love for Him and for our fellow men. Our giving is an expression of love and an act of praise and worship to God.

Recognizing God's Ownership – From the Perspective of Creation

God created the world and the inhabitants of the world, thereby making Him the de facto owner of everything.

For by Him all things were created that are in heaven and that are on earth, visible and invisible, whether thrones or dominions or principalities or powers. All things were created through Him and for Him.

Colossians 1:16

When we come into the realization that God owns everything that we currently possess or will ever possess, it puts things in a very different perspective; it humbles us.

Our God is a munificent God (James 1:17, Romans 12:6-8). Because He loves us, He gives and He keeps on giving to us (John 3:16). The Greek word used in John 3:16 for give is *didomi*[2]. When translated literally it means, "of one's own accord (free will) to give one something, to his advantage." Therefore God of His own accord or free will gives us things to our advantage. God supplies our needs of His own free will.

Putting it all together, it means that by the grace of God we acquire everything we own. It is not "my" car but the car God has freely entrusted to me; not "my" money, but the ability to earn money God has freely entrusted to me; not "my children", but the children God has freely entrusted to me. You may say, wait a minute, my children are my flesh and blood; but the Bible says, *Behold, children are a heritage from the LORD* (Psalm 127:3).

Our spiritual experience is not only related to a deep knowledge of the Bible, regular attendance to church, clear exposition and teaching of His word, and lengthy times of prayer and prominence in the Lord's work; these things are all very commendable. However, our adherence to the principles of stewardship and the way we relate to God and our fellow men with our possessions (money, time, talents) are very important aspects of our spiritual relationship with God (Matthew 6:21).

In order to give willingly to God and to His cause, an individual must be in love with God. It doesn't matter how many sermons an individual hears about stewardship or how many seminars he or she attends, if the love of God is not in that individual's heart he or she cannot respond of "their own accord". Such individuals find great difficulty in giving a gift to God, since they do not see their possessions as belonging to Him. These individuals act as if everything they have been entrusted with belongs to them.

The Comptroller of the Central Bank of New York has been entrusted to look over the bank's funds. If that individual begins to act as if the monies in the bank were his or her own, then he or she would be very much inclined to try to steal or swindle the bank's monies; that would be considered a federal crime. The individual would have broken the law and would be subject to the penalties thereof. By the same token, when individuals act as if they own the things that God have entrusted to them, they would be stealing or swindling from Him (Malachi 3:10). Those individuals would also have broken the seventh commandment (Exodus 20:15).

When we fail to recognize God's ownership, we are elevating ourselves as God. Elevating oneself to the status of God is a sin of pride. God detests a proud heart (Proverbs 6:17; 16:18). That was how the devil approached Eve in the Garden of Eden, suggesting that if she acquired God's portion she would be like God (Genesis 3:5).

Too often Christians have been conditioned to think that the only time they really need to get serious about giving is when there is a need that appeals to their particular emotion. And some needs seem more appealing than others, don't they? The Bible teaches that we are to give based on our love for God and not in response to our emotions or feelings (1 Timothy 6:17-19).

God lets us breathe His air, drink His water, bask in His sunshine and ski in His snow, all of which we enjoy but none of which we own (Psalm 24:1). And the beautiful part of it is that God never sends us a bill for our use of His creation. Imagine if you received a bill for God stating, "You've breathed 25 lbs. of air this week, and you owe Me X number of dollars." God never sends us a notice that our payment is past due, so we get no air this week. What a different picture life would be if God didn't love us with an everlasting love (2 Thessalonians 2:16).

The point is that none of us could live even for a second on this earth if God didn't abundantly share His wealth with us. Stewardship teaches us to respect God's property and to cherish what He has done and continues to do for us.

Recognizing God's Ownership – From the Perspective of Redemption

The devil tried to cut a deal with Christ (Matthew 4:9); if Christ would worship the devil, he would return the earth back to Him. Christ rebuked the devil and instead chose to redeem the world by dying on the cross. Christ now not only made us but He redeemed us back to Him. He not only created man but now He had also paid the price to re-create man (1 Corinthians 6:20). When a verse in the Bible begins with the word "For", it literally means, "it is a matter of fact." Therefore, a translation closer to the original Hebrew would read, *"It is a matter of fact that you were purchased with a price."* This is a reaffirmation that we are God's property (1 Corinthians 7:23). His purchase of us from the devil requires us to serve Him and to respond positively to His love.

If we want to have a meaningful relationship with God, it is of paramount importance that we accept God's ownership and follow His principles of stewardship.

Responding to God's Ownership

Establishing God's preeminence and His ownership in our minds are two necessary and sufficient conditions for understanding the true spirituality of stewardship. Once an individual understands and accepts that God is the owner, he or she is faced with two (2) choices for responding:

    (a) Choose not to accept God's ownership, and continue to steal from Him.

    (b) Choose to accept God's ownership and allow the Holy Spirit to lead him or her towards obeying the principles of stewardship.

Even though God allows us to voluntarily choose our response to His principles of stewardship, He provides some guidelines to assist us in our decision making process (Colossians 3:23). He also provides some warnings against disobeying them. Such warnings can be found in James 5:1-6:

> *Come now, you rich, weep and howl for your miseries that are coming upon you! Your riches are corrupted, and your garments are moth-eaten. Your gold and silver are corroded, and their corrosion will be a witness against you and will eat your flesh like fire. You have heaped up treasure in the last days. Indeed the wages of the laborers who mowed your fields, which you kept back by fraud, cry out; and the cries of the reapers have reached the ears of the Lord of Sabaoth. You have lived on the earth in pleasure and luxury; you have fattened your hearts as in a day of slaughter. You have condemned, you have murdered the just; he does not resist you.*

Dishonesty is defined as acts of lying or cheating or stealing. Therefore, dishonesty against God occurs when we refute His ownership.

The question can be asked, "is it possible to rob God?" The question was certainly on Israelite's minds during the time of Malachi (Malachi 3:8-12), when they asked; "How have we robbed you?"

It is to be remembered that everything belongs to God, and man belongs to Him too. He is the Creator, the sustaincr of all things. Everything is under His ownership. Psalm 24:1; *The earth is the LORD's, and all its fullness, The world and those who dwell therein.* God claims the first fruit of the harvest (Leviticus 23:10-14). He has claim to a tithe of all man possesses including time, energy and service, as well as possessions (Leviticus 27:30-32).

In the New Testament His claim on us is unchanged; if anything because we have received more we should be willing and able to give more. To withhold is to rob God [Malachi 3:8-12]; "Will a man rob God? Yet you [have] robbed me. But you ask; How do we rob you? [You have robbed me] in tithes and offerings. It may be unintentional, but that does not alter the responsibility. God is robbed in our defective generosity, giving to other things before tithing in the local church. Malachi 3:10 says to "bring the whole tithe into the storehouse".

God is robbed in the lack of responsibility toward Christian ministry, for He says that "a laborer is worthy of his hire" [Luke 10:7 KJV]. God is robbed in our failure to maintain his work because of a lack of support both practically and financially. If we are not supporting God's church by our commitment to be present when possible, to pray for the ministries, to support the programs of the church or by personal invitations to others, God is robbed.

God is robbed when our times in worship and our times in the word of God are abbreviated or all together neglected. Are we honest with our time, our possessions, our abilities, our privileges, our friends? This dishonesty in holy things is a trespass for which God requires amends and restoration.[3]

God encourages us to enjoy fully the possessions that He has entrusted to us, but we must remain cognizant of the fact that He is the owner and He is in control (Exodus 34:14). When we understand that we are His stewards, our attitude and our motive in responding to God's love are aligned with His will for our lives. As true stewards, we do not question why we need to bring a gift to the altar; instead we seek every opportunity to bring a gift to the altar so that God can use it to benefit others.

God loves us and He will do for us whatever it takes to makes us successful in our lives. Giving to God must be voluntary, but when we choose to give to Him, He requires of us our best. He will find our sacrifices to be acceptable to Him if we follow His principles for stewardship.

Why Did God Specify Ten Percent?

It is not the intent of this author to get involved in the debate of whether the ten (10) percent tithe was abolished with the Mosaic Law (under the Old Covenant) when Christ died on the cross, or whether it is supported in the New Covenant that is defined in the New Testament. Having said that, a prayerful study of God's word would lead you to discover that while the Old Testament focused on tithing at ten (10) percent, the New Testament took the concept of giving to God to a new spiritual level. The New Testament writers expanded the concept of giving to God to include giving everything the individual could possibly give, and that included the entire body as a sacrifice to God (Matthew 13:44, Matthew 19:16-21, Matthew 25:15-48, Luke 12:58,59, Luke 21:1-5, Acts 4:32-37).

I would like to keep the focus of this thought to the more fundamental question - why did God specify a quota or the ten (10) percent?

Why in the Bible does God instruct worshippers to bring a sacrifice of their own free will (Leviticus 1-5, 2 Corinthians 8:12, 2 Corinthians 9:7, Ephesians 6:5-7), and then in other places it appears that He established a fixed number – ten (10) percent (Genesis 14:17-20; Genesis 28:20-22; Leviticus 27:30-33; Malachi

3: 8-10; Matthew 22:21; Hebrews 7: 1-10)?

Before we begin to define the answers to the above questions, let's review God's objectives for the worshipper who follows the principles of stewardship:

1. Provide the worshipper with the opportunity as well as a mechanism to systematically and regularly express his or her love for Him (Matthew 22:37).
2. Provide the worshipper a mechanism to demonstrate his or her acceptance of Christ as the example of a faithful steward (John 3:16).
3. Allow the worshipper an opportunity to demonstrate that he or she recognizes God as owner and provider.
4. Allow the worshipper to demonstrate his or her acceptance and realization that he or she is in a covenant relationship with God.
5. To allow the worshipper to demonstrate his or her desire to come close to God (Ephesians 2:13).
6. To allow the worshipper to demonstrate his or her acceptance of the death of Christ on the cross as his or her sacrifice.
7. By using the offering to support the promulgation of the gospel, God allows the worshipper to participate in the divine plan of salvation and redemption of the world.

However, we have one small problem called "human nature" that gets in the way of our following God's guidelines. Adam and Eve had problems establishing the ownership of God in their minds; this was one of the problems that we inherited from them. As we review the history of the existence of man on this earth, we find God establishing very specific guidelines for the human race (for example the Israelites) so that they could become examples of faithful stewards to the world.

If we, as God's people, had fervently followed His principles of stewardship, we would not have experienced as many problems as we do today in funding and promulgating His work; the gospel would have reached all the ends of the world and God would have already returned and our assignment on earth would have been completed (Matthew 24:14).

We have demonstrated that our human minds have great difficulty understanding the concept of God's portion. The same questions we ask today were asked throughout the ages:

- Is God's portion ten (10) percent or is it fifteen (15) percent?
- Should I give from my net or from all of my increase (gross)?

Once again in His love for us (agape love is patient), God established a number to help us grasp the concept of His portion. If the worshipper gave ten (10) percent along with a free will offering, God would consider that as a "memorial portion" (Genesis 14:20); this act would signify that the individual had reserved God's portion. The human mind now had a specific number to assist us in understanding God's portion.

It was not God's original intent to assign a specific number to His portion; that allocation was to be determined by the individual's love for God. The Pharisees took a very exact and legalistic approach, thereby restricting the individual to the quota and missed the fact that it's all about our love for God and our fellow men. Jesus chided them for that:

> *Woe to you, scribes and Pharisees, hypocrites! For you pay tithe of mint and anise and cummin, and have neglected the weightier matters of the law: justice and mercy and faith. These you ought to have done, without leaving the others undone. Blind guides, who strain out a gnat and swallow a camel!*
>
> Matthew 23: 23,24

To bring this concept closer to everyday life, let's review the concept of driving safely. The desired objective of driving safely is to minimize the risk of accidents and related injuries or even death. When individuals apply for a driver's license, they go through a process of learning several guidelines whose sole purpose is to yield vehicle operators who know how to drive safely.

Statistics from the Automotive Service Association (ASA) show that 21.5 percent of registered vehicles in the United States are involved in collisions each year. In 2000, the estimated number of registered cars and light trucks in the United States was 215,794,435, giving an estimated 46,395,803 vehicular accidents that year. Of those near 46.4 million accidents, 3,247,706 cars and light trucks wound up totaled. The statistics indicate that we are having problems comprehending the concept of driving safely.

In order to help us better understand that concept, lawmakers have established strict speed limits for the roads, especially those that have the highest occurrences of accidents. On most major roadways the speed limit established for driving safely is 55 mph. Therefore, the concept of driving safely has a number attached to it. It has been quantified so that the human mind can grasp the concept of driving safely.

If an individual is driving at 55 mph, that person is considered to be driving safely; however if the individual is driving at 60 mph in a 55 mph zone, that person is considered to be driving unsafely or recklessly and have broken the law. Now very simply the human mind can comprehend the concept of driving safely (no more than 55 mph) so as to achieve the desired objective of minimizing the risk of accidents and related injuries. Smart drivers know that driving safely is not only driving below the 55 mph speed limit; they know that it includes being alert, being aware of what's happening in front, at the side of, and at the rear of their vehicles.

Just as the authorities had to quantify or establish a quota to help us understand the concept of driving safely, God had to quantify or establish a quota (10 percent) to help human beings understand the concept of "God's portion". But like the smart driver who knows that driving safely is not driving only below the established 55 mph speed limit, a wise Christian knows that stewardship is not restricted to returning only ten (10) percent to God.

It is God's desire that we respond to Him in love. Everything we do must be based on love, love for God and love for our fellow men. Love is not quantifiable nor does not establish quotas. When we go to the store to purchase a gift for someone we truly love, do we find ourselves establishing a price tag on it? Do we say to the store manager, "what gifts would you recommend for someone I love ten (10) percent or fifteen (15) percent?" Instead, we purchase the best we can afford for the individual we love. However, when it pertains to the God of the universe, our sustainer, our provider, why is it that we entertain the concept of a ten (10) percent gift?

The motivating factor behind a successful relationship with God must be love; in every aspect of our Christian life love must provide the stimulus for our response to Him. When love motivates our adherence to His principles of stewardship, our response to Him is no longer dictated by a quota but by a desire to demonstrate our deep and sincere love for Him.

The Bible says in 2 Corinthians 9:7:

> *So let each one give as he purposes in his heart, not grudgingly or of necessity; for God loves a cheerful giver.*

When Paul says "*as he purposes in his heart*", he means every worshipper as he prefers or as is his desire based on his love for God. We are not to allow anyone to dictate our response to God. Paul continues, "*For God loves a cheerful giver*", the Greek word for cheerful is **hilaros**[4], the root of the English word hilarious. Therefore, God loves the worshipper who takes great pleasure in giving or one who enjoys the act of giving and who takes no thought in how much the gift is worth, only that his or her gift pleases God — as a sweet aroma unto Him (2 Corinthians 8:12). This applies to the way we relate to God in all aspects of our life, our time, our talents, our possessions, including our bodies (Romans 12:1).

Stewardship represents a lifestyle change for many of us since it requires us to first sincerely analyze our relationship with God (Luke 10:27).

Giving Willingly Requires Motivation by Love

God promises a blessing for all those who give willingly (Matthew 6:32-33, Acts 20:35, Malachi 3:8-10, Psalm 41:1, 2 Corinthians 9:6-11). However, the motive for a free will gift to God should not be the fact that a blessing has been promised to the giver.

God is not a man that He should lie (Numbers 23:19), so those who give with the correct motive will be blessed. God blesses the giver in proportion to how much he or she has given. As our love relationship with God expands and we learn to obey Him more and more in our daily adherence to the principles of stewardship, He blesses us accordingly. Jesus admonishes us;

> *Give, and it will be given to you; good measure,*
> *pressed down, shaken together, and running over will*
> *be put into your bosom. For with the same measure*
> *that you use, it will be measured back to you.*
>
> Luke 6:38

One could rationalize that because of this promise, if I gave God ten (10) percent, He will open the storehouses of heaven and bless me with thirty (30) percent, so my ninety (90) percent would be increased to one hundred and twenty (120) percent. Such rationalization is not in the spirit of true stewardship but of the mindset of a Wall Street investment banker. God is displeased with such an approach to stewardship since it focuses more on the materialistic than on the spiritual. The word of God says (John 4:23, 24) that the worshipper's motivation for their sacrifice to God must be love; love for God and for their fellow man. He uses the offering to further the work of the gospel and to help supply the needs of others less fortunate amongst us. Paul provides this counsel in his letter to Timothy:

> *Command those who are rich in this present age not*
> *to be haughty, nor to trust in uncertain riches but in*
> *the living God, who gives us richly all things to*
> *enjoy. Let them do good, that they be rich in good*
> *works, ready to give, willing to share, storing up for*
> *themselves a good foundation for the time to come,*
> *that they may lay hold on eternal life.*
>
> 1 Timothy 6:17-19

God Is a Just God

One day Jesus told the crowd who had gathered around him a very interesting story, recorded in Matthew 25:15-28. It involves a master and three of his servants whom he left as stewards of his possessions. The master divided his possessions amongst the servants, giving each one according to his ability to manage the possessions. The master left the servants to be the stewards of his property. When he returned from his journey, he would determine who had demonstrated the characteristics of a faithful steward.

None of the servants received more than they could manage. To one servant, he allocated five (5) talents, to another two (2) talents and to the last one a single (1) talent. Then the master left and went on his way. While he was away, the servant who had been assigned the five (5) talents invested them and he received five (5) more for a total of ten (10) talents. Likewise, the servant who had been assigned two (2) invested them and he received two (2) more for a total of four (4) talents. The servant who had been assigned the single talent failed to use it or invest it and as a result did not receive an increase in his allotment.

One day the master returned and did an audit of the servants, he discovered that two of the servants had invested their allotments and had doubled the original assignment. The servant who received the single talent failed to invest his and instead he scolded the master for being unfair to him. The master was pleased with the two servants who had invested his possessions, pronouncing on them the title of faithful stewards. He was very displeased with the servant who did nothing with his assignment and scolded him for being an unfaithful steward. He then took his allotment and gave it to the servant who had ten (10) talents, giving him a total of eleven (11) talents. Because of his untrustworthiness, the last servant ended up with nothing.

In this story, the master symbolizes Jesus and the three servants signifies two types of Christians: one type of Christian is the one who practices the principles of stewardship, the other type ignores them. The possessions the master left the servants represents the things (skills, possessions, money, influence, etc.) that God has endowed us with.

In Jesus' day, a talent was currency used by the Roman Empire; it was worth six thousand (6,000) denarii. A day's wages, on average, was one denarius. Using a three hundred and sixty days business year, which is the same as the number of days in the Jewish calendar year of that time, six thousand denarii was more than the salary earned over sixteen years. Therefore, the servant who was given the one talent had more than enough to take care of his needs had he invested it correctly. He chose not to invest his talent, but to bury it.

God gives each of us a head start in this life. When we were born into this world, God endowed each of us with resources He deemed necessary for us to be successful individuals; as we go through life, the choices we make determine whether we invest those endowments or squander them. Unfortunately, some of us squander our head start because we find ourselves comparing what God has given to us to that which He has given to another.

The servant who was given five talents committed all, and the master endowed him with five more; the master adjusted his increase to match his commitment. God adjusts our prosperity to match our commitment to His principles of stewardship; the more we are committed to obey them the more He blesses us. God gives to each "in proportion to their ability" to manage His assets. The other servant, who was given two talents, committed all and he was rewarded with two more. The servant who received one talent refused to commit anything; he committed zero.

Our attitude towards God determines our gratitude towards Him. The servant who had the one talent also had the worst attitude towards his master; as a result his gratitude was the least. Now we understand why God could not have entrusted this servant with more; he was an unfaithful steward. The master took his talent and gave it away so he ended up with zero. Once again the master adjusted this servant's increase to match his commitment. God adjusts our increase or blessing to match our level of commitment because He is a just God. (Luke 6:38, Luke 12:48).

It is also interesting to note that because God is ultimately interested in our salvation, He never gives us more than we could bear (1 Corinthians 10:13) and that includes giving us more possessions that we are able to manage; if he did, we would lose our soul salvation. In other words, God doesn't give to us more that we could manage and still remain faithful stewards.

The master pronounced the title of faithful servant on two of the three servants when he returned from his journey. God has given us the time, talent and possessions to use for the benefit of others until He returns. When He returns the second time, He will conduct an audit to determine to what extent we have used our possessions and increases to promote His work and to benefit others. If during His absence we followed His principles of stewardship in our lives, He will confer on us the title of faithful steward; if we did not, we would receive the title of unfaithful steward and be cast into hell.

My Sacrifice Motivated by Love Benefits Others as Well as Myself

There is a text in Matthew 6:20 that I read and interpreted at face value for many years. It says:

> *but lay up for yourselves treasures in heaven, where neither moth nor rust destroys and where thieves do not break in and steal.*

One day while doing some research for a stewardship seminar, God revealed to me a second text in Philippians 4:16-18;

> *For even in Thessalonica you sent aid once and again for my necessities. Not that I seek the gift, but I seek the fruit that abounds to your account. Indeed I have all and abound. I am full, having received from Epaphroditus the things sent from you, a sweet-smelling aroma, an acceptable sacrifice, well pleasing to God.*

Because it is the inspired word of God, the Bible interprets itself, so the second text in Philippians explains further Christ's statements in Matthew. Our accounts are in heaven; whatever we give or sacrifice on earth, provided it is motivated by our love for God, is credited to our accounts in heaven. Every good deed we do on earth is credited to our accounts in heaven; therefore, we are laying up our treasures in heaven, the place where it matters the most. Unlike the uncertainty of the earthly banking system, our deposits in heaven are guaranteed through Jesus Christ; He is our guarantor (Ephesians 1: 13, 14).

God does not need our gifts. He uses them to meet the needs of others, thus adding fulfillment and purpose to our lives on this earth.

> God gives us gifts not just for our own enjoyment, but also so we can help others. "As each one has received a special gift," 1 Peter 4:10 explains, "employ it in serving one another, as faithful stewards of the manifold grace of God." We need each other, and when we use our gifts to help others, we provide them with a tangible example of God's grace and goodness toward them.[5]

God created us with a choice as to how we respond to His love. We can choose to allow the Holy Spirit to motivate us to respond in love or we can choose to allow the devil to control our human nature. When the devil is allowed to control our response to God's love, greed takes over. When greed takes hold of our lives, we find ourselves with an insatiable appetite for more and more material possessions. We lose the desire to return God's portion, and if we do, it is done grudgingly. An individual who is controlled by greed cannot experience happiness and fulfillment in his or her spiritual life.

When we willingly follow the principles of stewardship, motivated by our love for God, He promised that He would bless us. When God blesses us, those around us benefit from our blessings as well. Therefore, when God blesses me for being a faithful steward, my family benefits as well; when He blesses my spouse and kids for being faithful stewards, I benefit as well from their blessings. When I am a faithful steward, those around me benefit from my blessings. It is a good thing to keep company with those who walk in the ways of the Lord (Psalm 1:1, 2).

True Stewardship Results in True Happiness

Some people falsely believe that they can acquire true happiness and fulfillment by acquiring much wealth. Jesus admonishes us about the fallacy of such a belief in Luke 12:15 when He said,
"Take heed and beware of covetousness, for one's life does not consist in the abundance of the things he possesses."

He then proceeded to tell them about the parable of the rich fool (Luke 12: 16-21) who allowed his greed to destroy him.

When the love of God is absent from the heart of an individual, that void is filled by greed. Happiness and true fulfillment in life are not achieved by the acquisition of wealth or money but in being a faithful steward of what God has left in our care. There are several rich and famous people who have come to that conclusion; consider the following statements from them:

> "Happiness comes from spiritual wealth, not material wealth... Happiness comes from giving, not getting. If we try hard to bring happiness to others, we cannot stop it from coming to us also. To get joy, we must give it, and to keep joy, we must scatter it."
> - John Templeton

> "If money is all that a man makes, then he will be poor — poor in happiness, poor in all that makes life worth living."
> - Herbert N. Casson

> "Money never made a man happy yet, nor will it. There is nothing in its nature to produce happiness. The more a man has, the more he wants. Instead of its filling a vacuum, it makes one. If it satisfies one want, it doubles and trebles that want another way."
> - Benjamin Franklin

"Most people have a wrong idea of what constitutes true happiness. It is not attained through self-gratification but through fidelity to a worthy purpose."

- Helen Keller

"I expect to pass through this world but once; any good thing therefore that I can do, or any kindness that I can show to any fellow creature, let me do it now; let me not defer or neglect it, for I shall not pass this way again."

- Stephan Grellet

"Let no one ever come to you without leaving better and happier. Be the living expression of God's kindness: kindness in your face, kindness in your eyes, kindness in your smile."

- Mother Teresa

"Unnecessary hustle is one of the American follies. We hustle at both work and play, and consequently enjoy neither to the utmost."

- William Feather

"If money is your hope for independence you will never have it. The only real security that a man will have in this world is a reserve of knowledge, experience, and ability."

- Henry Ford

Final Thoughts

When we adhere to the principles of stewardship, we must allow the Holy Spirit to bring us to the realization that we have been entrusted with God's property; returning God's portion becomes natural to us once we have the love of God in our hearts. Stewardship takes on a deep spiritual significance to us, when we set God first in our lives.

There is no concept of volunteerism in stewardship. When we present our gifts (time, talent, influence, etc.) it is an opportunity God gives us to participate in His work; an opportunity for which we should be grateful and excited.

Our worship of God must precede our gifts to Him. True worship begins with a deep respect and reverence for God; it is the result of a new heart and a new attitude in us (2 Corinthians 5:17).

Like the sign in the window of a recently re-opened store read, "We Are Under New Management", we must come under God's management before we can learn to effectively manage His property. In Matthew 2:11, we read that the Magi or wise men first worshipped the child, Jesus, before they presented their gifts. God must be first in our lives before we can practice His principles of true stewardship; stewardship then becomes an integral part of our worship experience.

True stewardship is a relationship with God that both receives and gives, allowing the individual to realize spiritual enrichment and fulfillment. True stewards recognize the sovereignty of God, and they devote themselves daily to the conviction that they, as Christians, reside in a state of duality: as a Child of God, their salvation is a gift from God, and as a steward, the Christian is a giver.

Our sacrifice to God does not only consist of our finances; it is our time, our talents, our influence or any of our possessions, mental or physical, that can be used by God in the furtherance of His work.

> I do not think I exaggerate when I say that some of us put our offering in the plate with a kind of triumphant bounce as much as to say: "There—now God will feel better!" ...I am obliged to tell you that God does not need anything you have. He does not need a dime of your money. It is your own spiritual welfare at stake in such matters as these... You have the right to keep what you have all to yourself—but it will rust and decay, and ultimately ruin you.[6]

Who we are and all that we have is God's gift to us; who we

become and what we do is our gift to God!

> "In the end that's what matters, how you live your life."
>
> - U.S. Senator Trent Lott, 2002.

References:

1. *What Is A Steward?* – S. Reginald Michael, Ph.D.
2. Greek #1325 – *Strong's Dictionary of Hebrew and Greek Words.*
3. *The Village Pastor's Simple Guide to the Offerings of the Tabernacle,* compiled from material in the following books:
   - *Dictionary of the Bible* by Grant & Rowley
   - *Expository Dictionary* by W.E. Vine
   - *Daily Bible Study* by William Barclay
   - *Expositors Bible Commentary* by Frank E. Gaebelein
   - *Ungers Bible Dictionary* by Merrill F. Unger
   - *Wycliffe Bible Encyclopedia* by C.F. Pfeiffer, H.F.Vos and J. Rea
   - *Thus Shalt Thou Serve* by C. W. Slemming
   - *These Are the Garments* by C. W. Slemming
   - *Made According to Pattern* by C. W. Slemming
   - *Hastings Bible Dictionary* by James Hastings
   - *God's Tabernacle in the Wilderness* by John Carter
4. Greek #2431 – *Strong's Dictionary of Hebrew and Greek Words.*
5. *Using our Time, Talents and Treasures for God's purposes.* - Susie Hilsman
6. *Christ the Eternal Son* - A. W. Tozer

And the LORD respected Abel and his offering, but
He did not respect Cain and his offering ...
Genesis 4: 4,5

7

Is God Displeased With My Offering?

The devil would like us to believe that God is eternally merciful and nothing we do could ever displease Him. That is as dangerous a ploy as when he conjures up in our minds images of God as a tyrant. God has established guidelines in His word for us to live by, and when we disobey them, we displease Him and we become subject to the consequences of our actions.

However, if we honestly repent, in His mercy, God is faithful and just to forgive us (1 John 1:9). That forgiveness does not necessarily mean that we are immediately exonerated from the consequences of our disobedience.

The Bible teaches that when God is pleased with our sacrifices He blesses us (Matthew 6:32-33, Acts 20:35, Malachi 3:8-10, Psalm 41:1, 2 Corinthians 9:6-11). It also teaches us that He can become displeased with our sacrifices and in those instances we are not blessed. Is it possible that God is displeased with my offering? What about my sacrifice, does it displease Him?

Satisfying the Objectives of True Stewardship

In the previous chapter, we discovered several key objectives that God designed for the worshipper who desires to follow the principles of stewardship.

When these objectives are satisfied God is pleased and He accepts the offering as a "sweet smelling savor". Then and only then the worshipper can enjoy a sweet communion with God. In addition God blesses the individual. Conversely, when these objectives are not satisfied during the practice of stewardship, God is displeased with the worshipper as well as the offering that he or she brought.

Our Desire to Dominate Our Possessions Displeases God

Let us prayerfully analyze Genesis 4:1-7. Adam and Eve instructed their children in the ways of God and taught them how important it was to observe the objectives of bringing a sacrifice before God.

In spite of their parents' teaching, we find that God accepted Abel's offering and rejected Cain's. Did God reject Cain's offering because he was a farmer? Nowhere in the Bible do we find God discriminating against anyone because of his or her occupation; in fact His disciples were from various backgrounds and vocations. His invitation is extended to everyone irrespective of his or her background (Matthew 11:28).

Did God reject Cain's offering because he brought a fruit offering, while Abel brought an animal offering? During our review of the Levitical system of offerings, we discovered that not all of the offerings specified by God were of flesh; some of the non-flesh offerings consisted of grain and meal. We also learnt that each offering or sacrifice was closely aligned to what each individual could have afforded; the more fortunate were required to bring the more expensive cattle or lamb offerings and the less fortunate brought the least expensive grain or meal offerings. God does not ask of us what we do not have to give, for to do so would make the task unachievable and create a reason or excuse for us to not comply. He simply asks that we give the best of what was bestowed on us, lest we are tempted to steal from another.

In Genesis 4:3 we read,

> *And in the process of time it came to pass that Cain brought...*

Translated more literally it means: when Cain felt like it, he brought an offering. That violated the objectives; his sacrifice wasn't regular or systematic and it was not motivated by his love for God. The New International Version (NIV) translation of verse 3 is closest to the original Hebrew and it reads,

> *In the course of time Cain brought some of the fruits of the soil as an offering to the LORD.*

This again hints at an improper motive, since he brought "some of the fruits". One of the objectives for the worshipper is that he or she gives of his or her best to God, not "some" of the rest. That shows that we acknowledge and respect God as supreme and as our provider. By not bringing of the best of his fruit crop, Cain showed disrespect for God; he demonstrated that God was not first in his life.

By contrast we read in Genesis 4:4,

> *Abel also brought of the firstborn of his flock and of their fat.*

Two key points are to be noted from this passage. First, Abel brought from the firstborn, signifying the best of his flock; secondly, he also brought the fat portions. Our analysis of the Levitical system of offerings revealed God's specifications that the fat be burnt on the altar as a sweet aroma unto Him. Since the fat signified the best parts of the animal, it symbolized that the worshipper had reserved his or her best for God. Therefore, Abel demonstrated that in his mind God was preeminent and that he recognized Him as the owner of all of his possessions, so he reserved his best for God. Abel showed his respect for an awesome God.

In second half of Luke 6:38, we read,
> *For with the same measure that you use, it will be measured back to you.*

Since Cain showed no respect for God with his sacrifice, in return he received the same measured back to him; God did not respect him or his sacrifice. Cain's motives for sacrifice were not based on love; he did not love God and he did not love his fellow man (1 John 3:12). The proof of his bad motive and attitude is found in Genesis 4:5-8. He became angry with God and with his brother; his anger led him to murder his brother.

The name Cain means "possessive"; his name reveals his character. The word possessive means manifesting the desire to own or dominate. Cain's actions revealed that he manifested a desire to own or dominate the things that God bestowed upon him; he neglected God's ownership of his possessions. Some may even argue that he was a religious man because he took the time to bring a sacrifice, but his religion was a half-hearted selfish religion that did not put God first. Cain's religion was based on convenience and self-righteousness. He did not recognize that he was a sinner in need of a savior, and that his sacrifice was a symbol of the One who would come to die for his sins on Mount Calvary. He did not recognize or understand the spirituality of true stewardship.

Cain could not participate in true stewardship because he lacked a relationship with God. When God spoke to him (Genesis 4:6), instead of speaking with God, he turned his back to God and spoke to Abel. His lack of communication with God signified the absence of a relationship with Him as well as his lack of recognition of the presence and preeminence of God in his life. If we do not have a relationship with God, we cannot adhere to the principles of stewardship. As a result of his lack of a spiritual connection with God, Cain's offering became an abomination unto God (Genesis 4:7). Cain robbed God. He felt unfilled or empty in his worship experience to the point of contempt.

Conversely, we observe that Abel recognized the authority of God. Because of his respect for God, he brought an offering of the firstborn of his flock and he reserved all the fat portions for God.

Abel gave his best to God. Again following the biblical principle in Luke 6:38, God rewarded respect with respect; He respected Abel and his offering. Abel felt fulfilled in his worship experience.

God does not require equal contributions from us because we are all endowed at different levels, like the servants with the talents, but he requires equal commitment from us. We must all give Him our best.

Unfortunately in every congregation there are some Cains and some Abels. In case you may be wondering why you may not have realized fulfillment in your worship experience, even though you may be giving to your congregation, I advise that you prayerfully analyze your stewardship practices to ensure that you are satisfying all the objectives of the worshipper. If Cain had engaged in earnest dialogue with God, he would have been shown why God was displeased with him. He would have been given an opportunity to correct his errant ways and the situation would have had a happier ending.

Huge Losses When We Play the Numbers Game With God

Let's review another instance in the Bible where we find the worshippers' sacrifices displeased God.

> *But a certain man named Ananias, with Sapphira his wife, sold a possession. And he kept back part of the proceeds, his wife also being aware of it, and brought a certain part and laid it at the apostles' feet. But Peter said, "Ananias, why has Satan filled your heart to lie to the Holy Spirit and keep back part of the price of the land for yourself? While it remained, was it not your own? And after it was sold, was it not in your own control? Why have you conceived this thing in your heart? You have not lied to men but to God." Then Ananias, hearing these words, fell down and breathed his last. So great fear came upon all those who heard these things. And the*

young men arose and wrapped him up, carried him out, and buried him. Now it was about three hours later when his wife came in, not knowing what had happened. And Peter answered her, "Tell me whether you sold the land for so much?" She said, "Yes, for so much." Then Peter said to her, "How is it that you have agreed together to test the Spirit of the Lord? Look, the feet of those who have buried your husband are at the door, and they will carry you out." Then immediately she fell down at his feet and breathed her last. And the young men came in and found her dead, and carrying her out, buried her by her husband.

Acts 5:1-10

God looks upon His system of stewardship very, very seriously, since it is so intricately intertwined with His plan of salvation for the human race.

> Brethren and sisters, if the Lord has blessed you with means, do not look upon it as your own. Regard it as yours in trust for God, and be true and honest in paying tithes and offerings. When a pledge is made by you, be sure that God expects you to pay as promptly as possible. Do not promise a portion to the Lord, and then appropriate it to your own use, lest your prayers become an abomination unto him. It is the neglect of these plainly revealed duties that brings darkness upon the church. Let the elders and officers of the church follow the direction of the sacred word, and urge upon their members the necessity of faithfulness in the payment of pledges, tithes, and offerings.[1]

Our acts of stewardship must not be compared amongst each other. Stewardship is based on a personal relationship between the worshipper and God. Christ must be our only example for true stewardship; once we begin to compare our giving to that of another, the devil uses this opportunity to implant greed and jealously in the hearts of the believers. We lose our focus on Christ and selfish motives take over. The result is that our worship and our sacrifice become an abomination unto God.

> When Ananias saw how greatly Barnabas (Luke 4:32-37) was admired by God's people for his giving, he was filled with envy. So he and his wife agreed to lie to God. (Hypocrisy is lying to God!) They made a great gift to the church, but their gift was an act of greed. They gave because they wanted recognition. At first glance they appear to have done a great thing. They sold a piece of property to help the church. They gave a handsome amount of money, perhaps much more than Barnabas had given. But God looks on the heart (1 Samuel 16:7).
>
> The gift Ananias and Sapphira brought revealed a graceless, greedy heart. They pretended to give all, when in fact they had given nothing. No one asked them to give anything. Theirs was an unwilling sacrifice, given only in a hypocritical pretense, a sham, a show, a mockery. Their gift was an act of covetousness and greed, not of grace and love. They hoped to gain by giving, to gain the applause of men! Their gift was an abomination to God (Luke. 16:15). Beware of covetousness and hypocrisy![2]

Once again, the thing that displeased God was the motive of the worshippers; it was not correct. Their experience did not satisfy the objectives that God designed for the worshipper who desires to follow the principles of stewardship. Their gifts became an abomination unto God.

Using Our Possessions to Gain Prominence Displeases God

There are many other instances in the Bible that highlight the worshipper's adherence to the principles of stewardship. The result was that his or her offering pleased God. We find such an instance recorded in Mark 12:41-44:

> *Now Jesus sat opposite the treasury and saw how the people put money into the treasury. And many who were rich put in much. Then one poor widow came and threw in two mites, which make a quadrans. So He called His disciples to Himself and said to them, "Assuredly, I say to you that this poor widow has put in more than all those who have given to the treasury; for they all put in out of their abundance, but she out of her poverty put in all that she had, her whole livelihood.*

The word treasury in the original Greek is **gazophalakion**[3], a place for storing valuables, a contribution box. There were thirteen (13) such trumpet-shaped receptacles in the temple. As the coins fell down the trumpet-shaped receptacles, they landed in the contribution box with a loud resonating sound. Everyone watched the rich ostentatiously deposit their large offerings, accompanied by the loud sound of the coins falling to the bottom of the coin box; it was quite a spectacle.

At first glance it would appear that the rich were abiding by the principle in Luke 12:48: *For everyone to whom much is given, from him much will be required.* However, their sacrifices didn't seem to catch the attention of Jesus; He didn't seem to be interested in or pleased with their offering. The reason is found in the first part of Mark 12:44, *"for they all put in out of their abundance."* The Greek word used for abundance is **perisseuo,**[4] which means of their excess, so they were not really making a sacrifice; their giving was not sacrificial. Their gifts bore no significance to them either spiritually or economically; their act of worship was analogous to that of Cain's. In the sight of Jesus, it was as if they were not giving, since they were exhibiting a "form of godliness" (2 Timothy 3:5).

By comparison, the widow unceremoniously approached the collection box and quietly deposited her last two mites. She had deposited two small thin copper coins, which didn't resonate as loudly as the larger heavier coins of the rich. While no one appeared to have noticed, her gift made the loudest sound in the courts of heaven, and it immediately caught the attention of Jesus. Jesus found her sacrifice to be pleasing in His sight. The reason for this is recorded in the second part of Mark 12:44: *"but she out of her poverty put in all that she had, her whole livelihood."* He declared to His disciples that she had put in more than all the rich men combined. In the sight of Jesus, the widow's sacrifice was analogous to the sacrifice that He was preparing to make on the cross for us. She gave all that she had, even her very means of living, just as He did for us. Her act of worship and her practice of stewardship were motivated by her love for God.

When God acknowledged the widow's mite, He was not pointing out her one act of giving but rather the result of her lifestyle of commitment based on her love for Him. This is what separated her from the other individuals who were merely following the ritual of depositing their gifts into the offering bowls.

Every time you present your sacrifice unto the Lord, whether it be a monetary contribution, using your voice to sing praises unto God, using your influence to benefit another, giving someone a good recommendation for a job, whispering a comforting word to cheer someone up or any other such act of stewardship, God requires that you do so in the spirit of humility.

Each act of sacrificial giving should be the result of a lifestyle of commitment based on our love for God. Whenever we find ourselves using our sacrifices to draw the praise and attention of men, God finds no pleasure in them and He is also displeased with us. God allows us to use our physical possessions to make a spiritual connection with Him, but only when our minds are spiritually connected with Him.

When the offering plate comes down your aisle, do you smile or do you cringe? According to George Barns, Christian pollster, about three out of four Christians cringe. We must be true and honest believers if God is going to accept and be pleased with our gifts. David expressed this idea in Psalm 51:16 and 17 when, after committing murder and adultery, he realized that God is not pleased with a token offering of sacrifice. Rather, God requires a broken and contrite heart:

> O Lord ...You do not delight in sacrifice, or I would bring it; you do not take pleasure in burnt offerings. The sacrifices of God are a broken spirit; a broken and contrite heart, O God, you will not despise (NIV).

God will accept our worship only if our motive is pure and based on love. God looks at the heart of the worshipper before He looks at the gift that he or she brought to the altar.

The Greatest Principle of Stewardship

Consider for a moment an individual who has committed a crime punishable by death and is incarcerated awaiting trial and final sentencing. To add to the agony, the individual further discovers that he can't afford the high price of bail or of a fine lawyer. But inexplicably, a member of the victim's family posts bail for the criminal, arranges a way out of the death sentence, and hires the best lawyer in the country to represent the criminal. All the criminal is required to do is to be genuinely sorry for the terrible crime and purpose in his heart never to do it again. The criminal is now free to go, with no criminal record. Finally, his benefactor then agrees to make the freed criminal an heir to his estate.

This may sound like a fantasy, but it is the story of salvation. The convicted criminal represents us and Christ is our advocate and benefactor. Imagine for a moment how that freed individual feels. There is nothing that he or she would not do for his benefactor; in his mind there is no gift that could match the gift of life that the former criminal now enjoys. That's how the New Testament writers viewed stewardship. Christ came as promised and died for the human race, freeing us from the penalty of sin. We no longer need the complex sanctuary system of offerings; there is no longer a need to find turtledoves or lambs or grain, no more altar burnings, etc. All we have to do is to be genuinely sorry for our sins and, by the grace of God, desire to do them no more (1 John 1:9). Because of Christ's sacrifice, not only are we free from the penalty of sin, but we are also given rights to the property of the King of Kings and Lord of Lords (Romans 8:17).

As the New Testament writers looked back on Calvary and began to truly understand the awesomeness of the sacrifice of Christ and what it truly meant, they became overjoyed and overwhelmed by the goodness of God; in their minds no gift could match that of Christ's (John 3:16), not ten percent, not twenty percent. They concluded that the minimum we could do to show our appreciation to God is for us to give our all to Him. Paul summarizes the New Testament writers' principle of stewardship in Romans 12:1:

> *I beseech you therefore, brethren, by the mercies of God, that you present your bodies a living sacrifice, holy, acceptable to God, which is your reasonable service.*

It extends stewardship beyond just giving God our best to giving Him our all; that includes our bodies, our souls and our minds. Giving our all to God is the least that we can do in response to His munificent love shown on Calvary. This new principle of stewardship is consistent with Jesus' command in Matthew 22:37: *"You shall love the LORD your God with all your heart, with all your soul, and with all your mind."*

When you and me, under the influence of the Holy Spirit, begin to comprehend the significance of what Christ did on this earth for us, how He became poor so that we might become rich (2 Corinthians 8:9), we, like the apostles, would come to the conclusion that the least we can do for God is to give Him our all, our entire body and all that we possess as a sacrifice to Him. We would realize that everything we are, or we have, is only as a result of Christ's sacrifice at Calvary. Because one man was willing to give up everything He had, every man and woman can now have something to call his or her own.

The apostles focused on the spiritual relationship between the worshipper and God. Once we come to the place in our Christian experience where the Holy Spirit is guiding our lives, nothing is too much for us to give to God. We can say like the apostle Paul, *"nor height nor depth, nor any other created thing, shall be able to separate us from the love of God which is in Christ Jesus our Lord"* (Romans 8:38,39). I become my sacrifice to God.

When the Holy Spirit brings us to the point where:

- we see God for who He is.
- we understand the significance of the sacrifice of Christ on the Cross of Calvary (Romans 5: 12-21) and how He secured our freedom from the bondage of sin. We, too, will arrive at the same conclusion as did the New Testament writers. The New Testament writers presented the greatest principle of stewardship:
- we love God, we must surrender our all (our body, our soul, our minds and our possessions) to be used by Him; all to Him we must freely give.

This is echoed in Jesus' statement to the Pharisees in Matthew 22:37, *"You shall love the LORD your God with all your heart, with all your soul, and with all your mind."* Stewardship is a lifestyle for the believer of Christ; it is not a series of good acts performed by the individual.

Final Thoughts

An important theme emerges from the biblical instances reviewed above, and it is that God requires us to give Him our best. We can only give God our best if we love Him; simply stated, our motive for worship must be pure. Giving God anything less than our best causes Him to become displeased with our sacrifice and with us (Hebrews 10:31).

Why does God require the best from us? If the only reasons that God required our best were that He is the creator and the owner of everything, He would be a very self-centered and self-serving God. The Bible says in Deuteronomy 32:11-14:

> *As an eagle stirs up its nest, hovers over its young, spreading out its wings, taking them up, carrying them on its wings, so the LORD alone led him, and there was no foreign god with him. "He made him ride in the heights of the earth, that he might eat the produce of the fields; He made him draw honey from the rock, and oil from the flinty rock; curds from the cattle, and milk of the flock, with fat of lambs; and rams of the breed of Bashan, and goats, with the choicest wheat; and you drank wine, the blood of the grapes.*

God reserves the best for us, so He asks that in our sacrifice we reserve the best for Him. The Bible underscores this again in Jeremiah 29:11 (NIV),

> *"For I know the plans I have for you," declares the LORD, "plans to prosper you and not to harm you."*

The things that would cause God to reject us along with our sacrifices are:

- If our motive is not correct and not based on love. He considers such an offering a sinful act because we dishonor Him by rejecting His principles of stewardship.
- If we do not recognize Him as the owner of our possessions. Our possessions have become our god (Exodus 20:3).
- If we don't give Him our best.

As the minds of the New Testament apostles began to grasp the real significance of the death of Christ and how much He lay on the line for the human race at Calvary, they realized that stewardship is a lifestyle for the true Christian. It requires us to partner with the Holy

Spirit so that He can constantly and consistently use our all (our bodies, our souls, our minds and our possessions) to the will of God.

Achieving the status of faithful steward is a lifetime experience for the true Christian. It culminates with the coronation of the saints at Christ's second coming. Therefore, when we become believers in Christ we begin our stewardship journey at the foot of the cross and it continues during our daily walk with Him (1 Corinthians 15:30,31). Every day we make choices that determine the end result of the journey. Some of us are still at the beginning of our stewardship journey. Like Adam and Eve, we are struggling with the concept of God's portion; we find ourselves desiring God's portion. Some of us have advanced to the stage where we are allocating a portion for God, but we have set a limit on it — maybe it's only ten (10) percent or fifteen (15) percent. Then again, some of us may have reached the stage of the New Testament apostles; that is, we more fully understand the awesomeness of God's love and mercy towards us. For those at that stage in the journey, the least that we can do is to give our all to God. God warns us against being judgmental of each other; He cautioned His disciples to let the wheat and the tares grow together until His harvest (Matthew 13:29,30).

References:

1. Ellen G. White - *Review and Herald, December 17, 1889, paragraph 9*
2. *Bible commentary on Luke 4:32-37* by Don Fortner
3. Greek #1049 – *Strong's Dictionary of Hebrew and Greek Words.*
4. Greek #4052 – *Strong's Dictionary of Hebrew and Greek Words.*

*But Jesus said, "Let the little children come to Me,
and do not forbid them; for of such is
the kingdom of heaven.*

Matthew 19:14

8

Teach Our Children True Stewardship

Children need Jesus just as adults do. It is important to teach our children, at a young age, the principles of stewardship. If our children are to become faithful stewards when they grow to adulthood, we need to train them in the principles of stewardship from a tender age. This admonishment is given to us in the Bible:

*Train up a child in the way he should go, and when
he is old he will not depart from it.*

Proverbs 22:6

New imaging technology used to study brain development has proven that a child's early years offers a unique window of opportunity to develop and nurture talent or latent tendencies; science has proven what the Bible says in Proverbs 22:6.

Parents must train their children to respect their little bodies as the temple of the Holy Spirit (1 Corinthians 6:19). The Greek word used for temple in this Bible passage is **naios**[1], which is from the root word "naio" – to dwell. Therefore God dwells in our bodies by the indwelling of the Holy Spirit. The Holy Spirit is no respecter of persons, age, race or sex, so if we train our kids to respect Him, He will dwell in them also (Acts 10:34,35). Parents should work with the church leaders to reinforce these truths in the home.

Once our children understand God owns them and their possessions and He dwells within them, they can begin to understand, at a very tender age, the concept of God's ownership of everything – a fundamental principle of stewardship. An additional benefit of children understanding God's ownership of everything is that they learn to respect others and their possessions; we can then begin to teach them the "Golden Rule" found in Matthew 7:12:

> *Therefore, whatever you want men to do to you, do*
> *also to them, for this is the Law and the Prophets.*

For children to understand the principles of stewardship, they must see their parents practicing them and putting God first in the home. Children have great difficulty in learning and practicing what they do not see in the home; parents must be faithful stewards if their children are to become faithful stewards. Parents shouldn't relegate their duty to teach their children about stewardship to the teacher in the church's children's Bible study class or to the teachers in the church's school; the teaching of the principles of stewardship must begin in the home. A good start would be to teach children to set aside God's portion from their allowances. Rather than the parents withholding the tithe and offering, teach the child to take out God's portion as soon as you give him or her an allowance. Let them participate in the offertory by putting their offering in the plates.

We Must Teach Our Children How to Be Faithful Stewards

a. God entrusts every person with certain **talents, skills and abilities**. The writer of Romans 12:6-8 addresses the varying gifts that Christians possess:

Having then gifts differing according to the grace that is given to us, let us use them: if prophecy, let us prophesy in proportion to our faith; or ministry, let us use it in our ministering; he who teaches, in teaching; he who exhorts, in exhortation; he who gives, with liberality; he who leads, with diligence; he who shows mercy, with cheerfulness.

Children should understand from a very early age that God bestows many different gifts and graces upon His children. We must encourage our children to embrace these differing abilities and perspectives and to celebrate the diversity that exists amongst the members of the Body of Christ. We ought to challenge children to exercise their abilities and talents as soon as they are able to do so.

b. God entrusts every person with varying amounts and types of **material possessions**. We read in 1 Timothy 6:17,18:
Command those who are rich in this present age not to be haughty, nor to trust in uncertain riches but in the living God, who gives us richly all things to enjoy. Let them do good, that they be rich in good works, ready to give, willing to share.

We must teach our children to be faithful stewards of their money. Young children are capable of grasping the concept of tithing. They should begin to tithe a portion of their earnings or allowance as soon as they begin to receive money of their own. Jesus asks His listeners in Luke 16:11:
If, therefore, you have not been faithful in the use of unrighteous mammon [money], who will entrust the true riches to you?

We ought to challenge our children with Jesus' warning in Matthew 6:19; they are not to store up treasures on earth but to lay up for themselves treasures in heaven.

Children should have a clear understanding of the fact that they do not own anything. God owns everything and He has entrusted them with the job of taking care of His possessions. We need to quote Luke 16:10 to them often:

He who is faithful in what is least is faithful also in much; and he who is unjust in what is least is unjust also in much.

c. God entrusts every person with the generous gift of time. We find this exhortation in Ephesians 5:16 (NIV):

making the most of every opportunity, because the days are evil.

God has not promised us any time except the present moment in which we are living. Children need to understand how to value every day that God allows them to live. We should teach them to view time as a precious commodity that must never be wasted. We ought to encourage them to strive to honor God every day of their lives. [2]

Final Thoughts
Helping Children and Youth Develop Good Giving Habits[3]

- Provide brief prayers of thanksgiving for children and youth to use with their offerings.
- Ask children and youth to make their own pledges and to tithe their own money [allowances].
- Encourage the participation of children and youth through a variety of gift giving opportunities, where they can lay gifts directly on the altar or on some other symbolic place.
- Meet with [the church's Bible instruction] teachers, fellowship group leaders, and weekday activity leaders. Provide them with information about the importance of good giving habits. Ask for ideas and support for helping children and youth.
- Provide opportunities for parents to learn ways of teaching consistent giving to their children.
- Emphasize consistency of giving.

- Ask for time during [Bible instruction] classes to teach youth about the congregation's financial needs, connectional giving, and tithing habits.
- Provide offering envelopes for children and youth.
- Encourage missional [foreign missions] giving as well as giving to the [local] church budget.
- Set up the financial giving records so that confirmed youth have their own records. Include them individually in all financial mailings.
- Ask children and youth for ideas to promote giving.
- Develop an ongoing plan of financial education for children and youth.

References:

1. Greek #3485 – *Strong's Dictionary of Hebrew and Greek Words.*
2. *How Important is Biblical Stewardship for Children?* - Dr. Don Dunlap, Pastoral Counselor
3. Mary Alice Gran is a Director of Children's Ministries for the General Board of Discipleship.

It is the heart that gives, the fingers just let go.
                                        Nigerian saying

9

Some Reasons Why Most Stewardship Programs Fail

Empty Tomb, Inc., a Christian service and research organization reported, the following trends:

> Giving has not kept up with income, however. Protestant denominations have published data on an ongoing basis throughout the century. In 1916, Protestants were giving 2.9 percent of their incomes to their churches. In 1933, the depth of the Great Depression, it was 3.2 percent. In 1955, just after affluence began spreading through our culture, it was still 3.2 percent. By 2000, when Americans were over 450 percent richer, after taxes and inflation, than in the Great Depression, Protestants were giving 2.6 percent of their incomes to their churches.

One of the conclusions from this data is that the stewardship programs in many churches have failed to motivate their memberships; this is an issue that church leadership across the country is struggling to address. For this trend to be reversed, our churches' stewardship programs must become vibrant and provide spiritual enrichment to the lives of their membership. The stewardship program is as important and vital to the life of church and its membership as the prayer and Bible study programs.

Additional statistics on giving revealed the following:

> Americans (population 278.4 million) collectively made $7.51 trillion in income in 2000 (David B. Barrett and Todd M. Johnson, "World Christian Trends AD 30-AD 2000," (Pasadena, CA: William Carey Library, 2001)). Total giving was $152 billion (Giving USA). Americans could have comfortably doubled their giving to $320 billion without any change in lifestyle (New Tithing Group).

Why didn't we double our giving? Why weren't Americans motivated to give more? There are many reasons for this lack of motivation on the part of individuals to give. One reason is that the religious organizations, which traditionally have benefited the most from individuals' contributions, have failed to deliver on their charter of using the funds to provide services to their communities. Secondly, our churches have failed to promote the principles of stewardship and have resorted to the fund-raising techniques of the corporate world; the public has become disengaged, and the result is that they are holding onto their possessions instead of sharing them with others.

In our society, people are obsessed with material wealth and they view it as a sign of accomplishment; therefore, practicing stewardship is not very popular amongst the believers today. A recent report from Giving USA 2000 showed that three years ago, charitable giving exceeded $190 billion; of that sum, only 43 percent went to religious organizations. That means that more funds were given to other non-profit organizations than to religious organizations.

Whenever there is a principle of God, the devil has always introduced a counterfeit to confuse us; he did this back in the Garden of Eden with Adam and Eve. The devil's counterfeit to stewardship is philanthropy. Philanthropy derives its meaning from the ancient Greek, philia (from the root word for love that is philio) and anthropos (meaning humanity); it means, love for humanity. Stewardship, by contrast, is a spiritual principle that is manifested in an expression of gratitude to God; it is motivated by godly (agape) love, and it is one of the mechanisms used by God to provide for the needs of others. The motivation of a philanthropist is fundamentally different from that of a faithful steward. Philanthropy is donor-centric and stewardship is Christ-centric. Philanthropy is inimical to the principles that Christian stewardship embodies. As believers, we should be leery of the great deceiver's counterfeiting methods. Philanthropy, when properly managed and guided by pure motives, can benefit a lot of people, but it must not be confused with or used as a substitute for God's ordained system of stewardship.

Some statistics from Empty Tomb Inc. on churches reveals the following:

- 90 percent have no stewardship plan.
- One-third of churches are under-funded.
- Since 1970, churches have experienced increased staff (fixed expense). One contributing cause is the declining size of a volunteer base of women with 74 percent of women now working outside the home. The ratio of staff to members has almost doubled since 1970 from 5:1000 to 9.5:1000.
- Only one-third to one-half of church members financially support their church.

These statistics embellish the fact that there exists a need to educate the membership and the leadership of our churches and religious organizations on the importance of stewardship in the Christian experience of the believer.

The Church Must "Walk the Talk"

The church is one of the last remaining symbols of communal congeniality in our world today. The charter of God's true church must be to welcome each and every individual in the spirit of (agape) love and to provide an environment that allows the fulfillment of Christ in the heart and life of every believer, irrespective of their social or economic status. This translates to a warm and caring church body. Since the church is comprised of individual members, it means that a warm and caring church is a collection of warm and caring individuals, who are all motivated by the love of God.

In a warm and caring church, individuals, whether members of the body or of the church's neighboring community, feel that they have a place at the welcome table; by extension, individuals feel that they are a part of the body of Christ (1 Corinthians 12:27). When such an environment exists in a church, then each member exists in the state of Christian duality: as a child of God, each member is a gift to the body of Christ, and each member is a steward, giving to the body proportionately. In such a church, the stewardship program is alive and vibrant, and the stewardship leader functions as a manager of God's stewards.

For a church to have a successful and evergreen stewardship program, the love of God must permeate the church from the pulpit to the last pew. Each member must feel a part of the body and understand how the body is benefiting its members and its immediate community. The church must have a positive agenda for fulfilling the needs of its members and its community. Too many churches focus on accumulating much wealth, *"bring ye all the tithes into the storehouse"* (Malachi 3:10 KJV), and fattening their bank accounts, while their members and the surrounding communities languish in great need. For such churches, God has a similar admonishment as that given to the rich young ruler, *"go, sell what you have and give to the poor"* (Matthew 19:21).

By contrast, how many times have you visited a church or become a member of a church that has a "cold" environment, where the church seems more like a social club for the elite? Such a church seems more focused on achievement of mundane goals (for example: resurfacing the parking lot, and repainting the walls, etc.) established by its leadership or some "prominent" members, rather than on the fulfillment and spiritual enrichment of the lives of its entire membership and surrounding community. In such a church, the stewardship program is either dead or on life support, since the membership does not feel connected to the body. If the membership does not feel connected to the body, then they are not connected with each other; if they are not connected with each other, it is because the individual members are not connected to God (John 4:23,24; Romans 5:9-10). In such a church, the leaders make numerous appeals for commitment on the part of the membership, but such appeals fall on deaf ears. The stewardship leader in a church like this cannot function.

Church Leadership Must Be Committed to Stewardship

The leaders of God's people function on His behalf, therefore their wills must be aligned with His will (Proverbs 3:6).

Christian leadership is in touch with God— Those engaged in the work of God cannot serve His cause acceptably unless they make the best use possible of the religious privileges they enjoy. We are as trees planted in the garden of the Lord; and He comes to us seeking the fruit He has a right to expect. His eye is upon each of us; He reads our hearts and understands our lives. This is a solemn search, for it has reference to duty and to destiny; and with what interest is it prosecuted.

Let each of those to whom are committed sacred trusts inquire: "How do I meet the inspecting eye of God? Is my heart cleansed from its defilement or have its temple courts become so desecrated, so occupied with buyers and sellers, that Christ finds no room?" The bustle of business, if continuous, will dry up spirituality and leave the soul Christ-less.

Although they may profess the truth, yet if men pass along day by day with no living connection with God, they will be led to do strange things; decisions will be made not in accordance with the will of God. There is no safety for our leading brethren while they shall go forward according to their own impulses. They will not be yoked up with Christ, and so will not move in harmony with Him. They will be unable to see and realize the wants of the cause, and Satan will move upon them to take positions that will embarrass and hinder.[1]

In order to have a successful and vibrant stewardship program in your church, the leadership of the church must believe, practice, and be committed to the biblical principles of true stewardship. The leadership must elucidate and live the biblical principles of stewardship; they are to be examples of faithful stewards to their constituents.

It is interesting to note that 85 percent of pastors are untrained in the theology of stewardship and have no books in their libraries on Christian stewardship, money, or giving. In addition, most of the church's leadership presents stewardship as a mechanism to raise funds. In the book *Behind the Stained Glass Windows* by Ronsvalle and Ronsvalle, the authors noted that 84 percent of the pastors and 89 percent of the regional officials responding to the Stewardship Project survey affirmed, "In most congregations, the goal of stewardship is defined as meeting the budget." Since the church's leadership has limited stewardship to raising money for the church's project, it is not surprising that the membership now perceives stewardship as being "all about money".

The lack of education and training on the importance of the spirituality of stewardship for church leadership, at all levels of the organization, has contributed to the failure of the stewardship program in most churches. Since stewardship is based on spiritual principles, the spiritual leader of the flock, the pastor, must understand them; he or she must appreciate the value of stewardship edification for the body of Christ and must personally play a role in enabling and sponsoring the stewardship program of the church. The pastor must be a model of a faithful steward.

The Offertory — An Opportunity

Every pastor has at least one opportunity each week, the offertory prayer, to teach his congregation

Christian stewardship. Ninety [90] percent of the pastors miss the chance. Most offertory prayers are dull repetitions of drab clichés. Sufficient time should be given by the pastor to prepare this offertory prayer. He will discover that these prayers can become one of the most meaningful and stimulating parts of his worship service.

It's peculiar how a dollar can look so big to you when it goes to church and so small when it goes for groceries. It is far more effective to have a child bring a 10-cent offering to church school, if that is a tithe of his allowance, than to bring a dollar, which is given to him by his parent for an offering.[2]

What Right Had God With Mammon?

No one can serve two masters; for either he will hate the one and love the other, or else he will be loyal to the one and despise the other. You cannot serve God and mammon.

Matthew 6:24

Many churches run their stewardship program in a manner similar to not-for-profit or corporate fundraisers. Fundraising is program-centric and project-centric; it emphasizes response to a crisis instead of an ongoing commitment. Spiritual enrichment of the membership is not one of the objectives of fundraising.

A lot of churches are turning to the secular model of fundraising, but what right has God with mammon? Fundraising may allow a church to meet its immediate financial goals, giving the membership a false sense of fulfillment or achievement. One of the important objectives of stewardship is to build a spiritual relationship between the worshipper and God, which is not inherent in the secular models of fundraising.

Fundraising also promotes recognition for acts of contribution and seeks to establish levels of donorship; this is counter to the principles of stewardship that focus on the motive of the giver and not on the value of his or her gift. The devaluation of the members to just a "donor level" during these fundraising campaigns devastates the fabric of the congregation, and it sows the seeds for discontent and competition amongst the members. Fundraising creates an environment of commercialism in the church, which displeases God; He drove the merchants out of the temple (John 2:16) because it had become too commercialized. Stewardship is holy and should not be tainted with commercialism.

Church leaders and members must do all that they can to encourage every worshipper to be a faithful steward — while making every effort to avoid the slightest appearance of preferential treatment of the purportedly "big supporters of the church". The Bible in 1 Samuel 16:7 cautions us to refrain from such practices;

> *For the LORD does not see as man sees; for man looks at the outward appearance, but the LORD looks at the heart.*

No matter how the leadership may try to present it or to "dress it up," God does not sanction fundraising. It kills the church's stewardship program and, ultimately, the spirituality of the church. Fundraising angers the Holy Spirit; it causes Him to flee from the congregation. The church and its leadership answer to a higher authority.

Beware of Personal Favoritism

In some churches, the leadership has allowed an environment to foster where the "big contributors" are given special treatment. They are elected to the "prominent positions" in the church and are reserved the choicest seats at the fellowship table. When such situations are allowed to be present in the church, it demoralizes the membership over time and creates a class structure similar to that in the secular society. God is not pleased with such an environment; the Holy Spirit leaves and the church's stewardship program dies a sudden death.

My brethren, do not hold the faith of our Lord Jesus Christ, the Lord of glory, with partiality. For if there should come into your assembly a man with gold rings, in fine apparel, and there should also come in a poor man in filthy clothes, and you pay attention to the one wearing the fine clothes and say to him, "You sit here in a good place," and say to the poor man, "You stand there," or, "Sit here at my footstool," have you not shown partiality among yourselves, and become judges with evil thoughts? Listen, my beloved brethren: Has God not chosen the poor of this world to be rich in faith and heirs of the kingdom which He promised to those who love Him? But you have dishonored the poor man. Do not the rich oppress you and drag you into the courts? Do they not blaspheme that noble name by which you are called? If you really fulfill the royal law according to the Scripture, "You shall love your neighbor as yourself," you do well; but if you show partiality, you commit sin, and are convicted by the law as transgressors. For whoever shall keep the whole law, and yet stumble in one point, he is guilty of all.

James 2:1-10

We Are Children of the Light

Most stewardship programs fail because the members are kept in the dark about the use of the church's funds. The members of God's church are children of the light (Ephesians 5:8), so they should not be kept in darkness.

The membership should be given proper information as to how their contributions are being used by the organization. The local church leadership should provide monthly or quarterly statements to the church body at large and not only to the board members or the board of trustees. The Bible reveals in 2 Corinthians 8, 9 that Paul provided details to the Corinthians as to how their funds were being used in spreading the gospel. This not only helped to provide a sense of fulfillment for them, it also served to reinforce their confidence in his leadership. It also motivated them to continue to contribute to the work, since they were seeing the positive benefits of their gifts.

When the church leadership keeps the membership informed of the details on how their offerings are being used, it reinforces their confidence and credibility in their leadership. Many stewardship leaders lose the trust of their congregation, which results in their inability to be effective leaders and the failure of the church's stewardship program. Keeping the membership informed also motivates them to continue to contribute to the work. Sharing information with the membership about the uses of the church's funds keeps the local church's stewardship program evergreen and vibrant. It adds a sense of fulfillment to the membership and strengthens their faith in the power of God to use their funds in miraculous ways.

The Stewardship Leader Is a Spiritual Leader of the Church

The stewardship leader must see himself or herself as one of the spiritual leaders of the church before the congregation can begin to view him or her in that manner. For the stewardship program of the church to be successful, the stewardship department and leader must not be aligned too closely with the goals and objectives of the Treasury and Finance departments.

The Treasury and Finance departments are necessary and important departments and should be staffed by dedicated spirit-filled individuals. However, they do not provide spiritual leadership for the church; they provide administrative leadership for the church. All throughout this book, we have reviewed the biblical principles and reasons as to why stewardship is a spiritual matter of the utmost importance to the salvation of each and every individual. Stewardship is a spiritual experience that results in the enrichment and fulfillment of the life of the believer; it is not to be confused with the administrative task of the church. Keeping the stewardship program spiritual ensures its success in the church. Under the guidance of the Holy Spirit, the stewardship leader must guard against the department being perceived or managed as the fundraising arm of the Treasury and Finance departments.

The stewardship program of the church should not use the tax incentives for donations to non-profit organizations as a means of motivating the members into giving an offering. On numerous occasions I have visited congregations and heard the leaders remind the members that their gifts are tax deductible. God does not sanction this approach to stewardship, and the offerings in response to such appeals do not rise as a "sweet smelling savor" before Him. Secondly, such appeals lose their effectiveness over time, resulting in the failure of the membership to realize the true blessings from God. This results in the failure of the church's stewardship program.

God did not design stewardship as a means of meeting the church's budget; it was designed as a mechanism for God to meet the individual and elevate him or her to a deeper spiritual experience.

You Receive Not Because You Ask Not

Many church leaders have great difficulty in advocating the needs of the church. From time to time the opportunity will arise when the leadership has to make specific request of the congregation to fulfill a specific ministry of the church; the apostle Paul did it with the early churches in Ephesus and at Corinth.

Many church leaders falter when advocating the needs of the church and do not clearly articulate the purpose for which the offerings would be used; as a result, the congregation does not respond appropriately. We must not assume that every member in the church understands that supporting the congregation is part of his or her obligation to the body of Christ. The church is a community of individuals at different levels of spiritual maturity all striving to make it to heaven. Some members are striving with the ownership of God, others with how best to respond to His love. In addition, most churches do not teach the principles of stewardship to new believers during the initial study of the church's doctrines. Therefore after joining the body, new members are not adequately prepared for this aspect of their Christian experience. In order to keep the church's stewardship program evergreen and vibrant, the leadership must clearly advocate the needs of the church and the purpose for which the offerings are to be used; *"When you ask, you do not receive, because you ask with wrong motives"* (James 4:3 NIV).

Final Thoughts

It is God's desire that each individual realizes spiritual enrichment and fulfillment by following the principles of stewardship. When the individual members are enjoying such an experience the church collectively realizes spiritual enrichment and fulfillment from its stewardship program. Leadership at all levels of the organization must be committed to stewardship and must come to the realization of its spiritual importance to the body of Christ; it is equally important to the life of the church as prayer and Bible studies. The church's leadership must be trained and educated accordingly; their personal salvation hinges on their practice of its principles in their personal lives.

A stewardship program that focuses on lining the church coffers with wealth or meeting the budget displeases God; it is doomed to fail.

References:

1. *Testimonies for the Church, Volume 5, p. 423* – E. G. White

2. *Stewardship Aids Leaders Trends Newsletter* - Editor Walter J. Waddell, III - Church Publishing Manager

The tithe (10 percent) can become an idol to set upon a pedestal to shine. It is often a dangerously tempting resting place rather than a minimal starting place. Much of the Christian community thinks of tithing as a high and lofty perch that only a few fanatical radicals have reached after years of struggle, rather than seeing it as the bottom or beginning place.

Don McClaren

10

Organizing for a Successful Stewardship Program

Leadership is challenging, and when you deal with spiritual matters you add another dimension described in Ephesians 6:12:

For we do not wrestle against flesh and blood, but against principalities, against powers, against the rulers of the darkness of this age, against spiritual hosts of wickedness in the heavenly places.

Stewardship is a spiritual matter of utmost importance to the body of Christ. We are called by Christ to be disciples and to make disciples of men (Matthew 28:19); once we respond to God's call to become a disciple of Christ then stewardship is no longer an option.

As the Holy Spirit transforms the body of Christ from membership to discipleship, He leads them naturally into the practice of stewardship.

In the Bible, the body of Christ is likened to a flock of sheep. It is important to note that the shepherd does not make sheep, but it is the sheep that make sheep. The leadership of the church must recognize that it is the Holy Spirit who will use the stewards in the congregation to make other stewards within the congregation. The stewardship leader functions as a steward of God's stewards. No one person can accomplish the work of stewardship in the church, not even the pastor. We must all play our part, working in partnership with the Holy Spirit to convict and convince men and women to become faithful stewards. When He does it, the conversion is real. The stewardship seminars and revival meetings are all important, but they are instruments used by the Holy Spirit; they do not replace the role or function of the Holy Spirit on the leadership team.

For a church to be vibrant and on fire for the Lord, the Holy Spirit must be the leader of the leadership team, not just an invitee or only requested when there is a crisis to be solved. The pastors are there to serve; under the direction and guidance of the Holy Spirit, they are to minister to the membership. If the Holy Spirit is not in charge of the leadership team, there is only one other person that fills the void – the devil. A lot of churches are proceeding merrily along not realizing that it is the devil, disguised as an angel of light, who is leading the leadership team.

Organizing for an Effective and Vibrant Stewardship Program

To achieve a vibrant and effective stewardship program, the stewardship leader must first dedicate himself or herself to Christ; he or she must seek the guidance of the Holy Spirit in all matters. He or she must be a believer in the principles of stewardship, prayerfully defined in this book. The stewardship leader must also practice what he or she teaches, which means his or her life must be an example of someone striving to be a faithful steward:

> *And above all things have fervent love for one another, for "love will cover a multitude of sins." Be hospitable to one another without grumbling.*
>
> 1 Peter 4:8,9

That means that the stewardship leader must work closely with the pastor and the rest of the leadership team to promote the spiritual principles of stewardship in the body of Christ. Stewardship is not a one-person show; for the stewardship program to be successful, everyone must be actively involved.

The second thing that the stewardship leader must do is to prayerfully enlist the help of others to form a stewardship committee. Depending on the size of the church, the committee should be kept to either five (5) or seven (7) members, including the leader; it is best to have an odd number of members for voting purposes. It is advisable not to add Treasury and Finance personnel to the committee, not that they aren't faithful stewards, but it helps to eliminate the stigma of "begging for money" that has plagued so many stewardship programs (Matthew 10:16). An active, praying stewardship committee is absolutely critical to a church; they provide ongoing edification and encouragement to the church members in the use of their time, talents and treasures for God.

The goal of the stewardship leader and the stewardship committee is to allow the Holy Spirit to use their efforts to permeate the principles of stewardship throughout the entire fabric of the church. They must work in unison to create an environment where every member in the church can begin to realize spiritual enrichment and fulfillment in his or her adherence to those principles. When each member is giving his or her all to the work of Christ, the body of Christ becomes a vibrant organization. God not only blesses each member, but He blesses the congregation in miraculous ways.

Responsibilities of the Stewardship Committee

1. Develop an ongoing education and training program that facilitates the edification of the members on the spirituality

of stewardship. This book is an excellent resource to use as a study guide for the membership.

2. Work closely with the pastor(s) and other spiritual leaders of the church to edify and encourage the members on the journey to true stewardship.

3. Pray for much patience and persistence and then pray some more. Developing, implementing and maintaining a vibrant stewardship program requires much prayer, much patience and much persistence on the part of the committee and the spiritual leadership of the church.

An individual's adherence to the principles of stewardship determines his or her eligibility for eternal life (Matthew 19:16-22). There is a constant spiritual battle that occurs within every member as he or she strives to overcome the human traits (greed and selfishness) and to submit his or her will to God. Each member progresses at a different pace, so the committee must pray for patience. The devil does not make it easy for an individual to get to the point, where he or she totally understands that all that he or she possesses belongs to God; this does not happen overnight (1 Corinthians 15:31).

The stewardship committee must realize that they are in a spiritual warfare over the salvation of every believer in the church (Ephesians 6:12). It is God's desire that every believer be a faithful steward of His property, but it is the devil's aim to see each one be an unfaithful steward, destined for hell. The good news is that the committee is on the winning side and is championing a worthy cause; they must prayerfully claim that victory.

4. Recruit individuals and/or couples to share their personal testimonies about stewardship with the membership. This helps encourage others and reinforces the principles of stewardship through experiential knowledge.

5. Ensure that those who volunteer for church activities are contacted and asked to become involved.

6. Evaluate the stewardship effort and awareness efforts on a regular basis, at least once a quarter.

7. Make every attempt to keep the message of stewardship in front of the people and use creative, but prayerfully developed, methods to do so. Remember, stewardship is a spiritual matter, so let the Holy Spirit lead the effort while the committee follows; He will guide you into all truth (John 16:13).

8. Publicize stewardship thoughts throughout the year in the church's bulletin, ideally on a weekly basis.

9. Make appropriate stewardship literature available in church booklet racks.

10. If your church has a newsletter, publicize stewardship reflections in it.

11. Work with the elders and pastors to incorporate comments about stewardship during the offertory. Use some of the principles presented in this book. Do not restrict yourselves to Malachi 3:8-10. Too many stewardship departments have used that passage of Scripture as a crutch for their program, and the membership has become insensitive to it

12. Add a children's stewardship component to your program.

13. Provide a continuing education programs for the stewardship committee.

14. Use external resources wisely to conduct stewardship seminars. Every time I conduct a stewardship seminar for an organization, I make every effort to involve the local leaders, since they are then ones who keep the momentum going after I leave.

15. Expand the focus of the church's stewardship program to include activities that benefit your local the community.

16. Work with the other church departments or auxiliaries to provide frequent financial and progress reports to the membership. Ensure that the members understand how their contributions (time, talent, finances and influence) are benefiting others both in the church and in the community. Provide sufficient details yet keep it confidential so that you minimize the risk of any legal ramifications.

17. Keep the stewardship program spiritual (Matthew 6:33); this is a matter of eternal life for all the believers, including

those on the committee.
Establish Goals and Objectives

We serve a God who is a master planner; He plans so well that He never needs a contingency plan. Before sin entered the world, God had the plan of salvation all worked out and ready to go. He expects us, as faithful stewards, to plan so that we do not fail.

He, who fails to plan with God, plans to fail without God.

Make your plans with God (James 4: 13-17), which is what separates our planning from that of the world; the world engages in presumptuous planning. As Christians we do not plan without God's direction.

The stewardship committee, working under the direct guidance of the Holy Spirit, with the pastor and the other spiritual leaders in the church, should prayerfully plan the church's stewardship program. The fundamental purpose of the church's stewardship program is to educate the membership on the spirituality of stewardship and to facilitate the fulfillment and enrichment of every believer's Christian experience — through stewardship. This can be used as the committee's mission statement.

I beseech the committee to plan prayerfully, since the devil loves to get involved in the planning of God's work; beware of egos and personal agendas. The stewardship leader must, at all times, keep God first and foremost within the committee (Matthew 6:33). Here are some suggested steps; you know your church's environment, therefore, let Godly wisdom abound:

Step 1: Analyze or Review Your Present Situation

a) What is the understanding of stewardship in your church? Is it limited to money? A good technique is to use a simple stewardship survey for the membership to provide their feedback. A sample stewardship survey can be found in the Appendix.

b) Are key stewardship lessons being taught to children, youth, young adults, seniors, in the various church's study sessions and from the pulpit?
c) Are there needs and opportunities for ministry that are not being addressed? Identify them and engage the appropriate auxiliaries to address them.

Step 2: Ask God to Set the Vision for the Committee

What does God want for the congregation in the area of stewardship? For example: Are all members of the congregation utilizing all of their God-given gifts all of the time in His work? Are the church's ministries flourishing with abundance of resources: people (time and talents) and material (money/building/equipment)? Ask God; He will reveal to the committee what is His desire for the church (Matthew 7:7).

Step 3: Plan and Set Goals

a) Set goals with the church's leadership; develop stewardship educational goals for all the Bible study sessions, youth programs, new believers, and seniors.
b) Work and track the plan; hold each person or group accountable for results.
c) One of the goals of the stewardship program should be to educate and motivate the membership to achieve spiritual fulfillment through adhering to the principles of stewardship.

Although finances are not the focus of the stewardship program, a successful program will result in increased participation and contributions from the membership. Once a church is meeting the needs of the members, both spiritual and physical, they will participate in and contribute to its programs. Stewardship is not talking, nor coaxing, the members out of their possessions; it is teaching them how to use them wisely to the honor and glory of God.

Step 4: Select a Stewardship Theme (preferably for the year)

Prayerfully select a theme for the year and stick with it; as the corporate guys say, "work the theme". Use various teaching methods, including the church's main Bible study sessions, small group Bible studies, preaching, drama, testimonials, displays, etc.

The stewardship theme should be closely aligned with the church's theme. For example, in a church where I served, one year the theme we selected for the church was "Possessing New Ground." That year the stewardship committee chose for their theme "Possessing New Ground Through Sacrifice." Therefore, every time the church's theme was mentioned it helped to reinforce the stewardship theme in the minds of the members.

Step 5: Review and Reflect

Evaluate: what works well or not so well? What should be repeated and how often? The plan is not something you develop and put on the shelf; if you desire to keep the stewardship program evergreen, then keep the plan evergreen, and revisit it during the year.

Step 6: Set New Goals

Pray for God's blessing as you set new goals, and hold people accountable.

Step 7: Plan a Stewardship Month

An entire month of stewardship emphasis will help in developing a giving church. When should you conduct it? It has been suggested by some stewardship leaders, based on their success, that January is one of the most effective months to conduct a stewardship emphasis. Since it is the beginning of a new year, people often find themselves making spiritual resolutions; making a resolution to regularly, and systematically, give to the church would be a good one to encourage.

Additionally, January is often one of the financial "slack times" and so an emphasis on giving is advantageous. Since people are beginning to prepare their income tax returns, it is a good time to help reaffirm the needs of the church and its ministries as members plan how to utilize their returns.

Step 8: Remember to Thank the Congregation for Their Support

In our Christian walk we must encourage each other (1 Thessalonians 5:11). A word of gratitude, offered at the appropriate time, is a very powerful motivator; that should not be confused with flattery. Secondly, we are human beings and we love to be appreciated, especially when we do good deeds; that is a characteristic we inherited from our heavenly Father (Psalms 150:1-6). Expressing sincere appreciation helps motivate the desired behavior in people; as a side benefit, it gives the committee a way to keep the stewardship theme in front of the people. Use every opportunity to express gratitude for the membership's ongoing support.

A tremendous opportunity arises when members donate (with stewardship there is no concept of volunteerism) their time or skill towards the completion of church projects: for example, church cleaning. At the completion of such projects, thank the members who donated their time or skill; let them know that it is credited to their account in heaven.

The end of the year, when the Treasury department is distributing the contribution reports to the congregation for income tax purposes, presents an excellent opportunity for the stewardship committee to include a thank you letter with the report. Depending on the size of the congregation, make every effort to personalize the letter for the individual or family; it really gets the message home. A sample thank you letter is included in the Appendix.

Some Thoughts on Stewardship for Leaders

The focus of this book has been to elucidate what the Bible teaches on the spirituality of true stewardship. Since our adherence to the principles of stewardship determines our eligibility for eternal life, we must present stewardship to each and every one as a spiritual matter of the highest importance.

It is my desire to leave you with a few key thoughts that you can use to assist you in presenting the principles of stewardship to your members. As you use them, allow the Holy Spirit to expand His truth in your mind and heart, so that He can assist you in motivating your congregation to become faithful stewards. Whenever you present these thoughts to the congregation, allow them to participate by reading the associated Bible verses. The stewardship committee should enlist the support of the elders, pastors and other leaders who participate in the main worship service to assist with presenting these thoughts. Working with the pastor and the other spiritual leaders, the stewardship committee should select a theme (monthly, quarterly or annually) for the stewardship program of the church. The thoughts presented each week should be aligned with the stewardship theme (1 Corinthians 14:40).

#1 - Realizing the Awesomeness of God Through Sacrifice

This thought is taken from Genesis 22:1-18; it reveals how we can achieve a higher spiritual relationship with God because He keeps on making a way for us. The concepts in this thought are best presented one concept at a time, probably at the time of the offertory, as a prelude to the offertory, or at the end of the collection of the offerings.

Thoughts from Genesis 22:1-18:

1. God is going to test (v1) the commitment and faith of each of us.
2. I, John Doe (allow each member to fill in his or her name) must be willing to achieve a higher spiritual relationship

with God through sacrifice (v1).

3. God is going to reveal to me what He wants me to sacrifice (v2).
4. In order to worship God and to demonstrate my love for Him, I must be willing to obey Him and to return a portion of what He has given me (v5) [John 3:16].
5. I must have faith in God and be willing to sacrifice whatever He asks of me, without questioning His reason (v5, 7).
6. God will be with me throughout my test of sacrificial giving (v11).
7. God will make a way for me, if I am obedient to His will (v12, 13).
8. John Doe (allow each member to fill in his or her name) is too "blessed to be stressed" as I go through this test of commitment and faith (v16, 17).
9. Because I am willing to make the sacrifice God asks of me, He not only blesses me, but the entire Doe's (allow each member to fill in his or her family name) family (v18).

#2 - Our Sacrifice Provides a Mechanism to Come Close to God

The Hebrew word for sacrifice, korban, comes from the root korav meaning to "come close," specifically, to come close to God. Our offerings were meant to bring us, who were separated from God because of sin, close to Him once again.

#3 - Extravagant Giving Is a Characteristic of God

Every good gift and every perfect gift is from above.
James 1:17

1. God gave us the world — Genesis 1 and 2.
2. God gives His Presence — Isaiah 41:10 "... I am with thee..."

3. He gives His Position... "I am thy God..."
4. He gives His Power... "I will strengthen thee..."
5. He gives His Partnership... "I will help thee... "
6. He gives His Perseverance... "I will uphold thee... "

Extravagant giving is a characteristic of God.
7. God gives His Love — 2 Timothy 1:6,7.
8. God gave us His only begotten Son — John 3:16.
9. God gave us eternal life — Romans 6:23.
10. God gave us children — Psalm 127:3-5.
11. God gave us the ability to enjoy the fruits of our labor — Ecclesiastes 3:13.
12. God gave us the Holy Spirit — Acts 8:18-20.
13. God gave us salvation through faith — Ephesians 2:8.
14. God is about to give us mansions in the sky — John 14:2: *In my Father's house are many mansions: if it were not so, I would have told you. I go to prepare a place for you.*

Extravagant giving is a characteristic of God, but extravagant spending is a characteristic of our human nature. However, in Philippians 2:5, we are commanded to be of the same mind which was in Christ. Therefore, we must allow God to bring our extravagant spending under His control. Then, as God's children, we will exhibit the characteristics of God, one of which is extravagant giving.

#4 - Give God the Best of What You Got — Part 1

Even as early as Genesis 4:3-5, offerings were mentioned in the Bible. Cain brought an offering to the Lord from the fruit of the ground and Abel brought the firstborn and its fat from his flock. The Hebrew/Greek word for the verb "to respect" can also be translated "to bless". God blessed Abel and his offering but rejected Cain and his offering. Why would God not bless me and, furthermore, reject my offering to Him. The answer is found in Exodus 13:11, 12 and in Exodus 23:19.

Exodus 13:11, 12

> *And it shall be, when the LORD brings you into the*
> *land of the Canaanites, as He swore to you and your*
> *fathers, and gives it to you, that you shall set apart*
> *to the LORD all that open the womb, that is, every*
> *firstborn that comes from an animal which you have;*
> *the males shall be the Lord's.*

Exodus 23:19

> *The first of the firstfruits of your land you shall bring*
> *into the house of the LORD your God. You shall not*
> *boil a young goat in its mother's milk.*

The lack of descriptive terms such as "firstfruits" for Cain's offering is conspicuous in its absence, especially in light of the description of Abel's offering as "fat portions" and "firstborn".

Cain brought an offering from **some of his fruit**, but Abel brought an offering **from the best of his flock**. We shouldn't pay the bills first, and then give God an offering from some of our leftover money — and expect to get a blessing. We must not give God an offering from what's left after paying the car note and the mortgage. God rejects such an offering and does not bless us.

The issue here wasn't that the offering must be of flesh since Levitical offerings were not only of meat but also of fruit and grain. God does not ask us to give of what we do not have but to give the best of what we have. After all, He was the one who gave everything to us.

#5 - Give God the Best of What You Got — Part 2

What does the offering of the fat of the animal mean in Abel's offering?

Leviticus 3:14-17:

> *Then he shall offer from it his offering, as an offer-*
> *ing made by fire to the LORD. The fat that covers the*
> *entrails and all the fat that is on the entrails, the two*

kidneys and the fat that is on them by the flanks, and the fatty lobe attached to the liver above the kidneys, he shall remove; and the priest shall burn them on the altar as food, an offering made by fire for a sweet aroma; all the fat is the Lord's. "This shall be a perpetual statute throughout your generations in all your dwellings: you shall eat neither fat nor blood."

The association of fat with the best is also revealed in the parable of the prodigal son in Luke 15.

Luke 15:20-24:

And he arose and came to his father. But when he was still a great way off, his father saw him and had compassion, and ran and fell on his neck and kissed him. And the son said to him, "Father, I have sinned against heaven and in your sight, and am no longer worthy to be called your son." But the father said to his servants, "Bring out the best robe and put it on him, and put a ring on his hand and sandals on his feet. And bring the fatted calf here and kill it, and let us eat and be merry; for this my son was dead and is alive again; he was lost and is found." And they began to be merry.

Fat denotes the richest part of the animal or the best of the flock; it denotes the best part of something.

Why does God require the best from us? You may say because He is God the creator. OK - that's true and you have heard that before, but there is another equally important reason:

Deuteronomy 32:11-14 (NIV):

Like an eagle that stirs up its nest and hovers over its young, that spreads its wings to catch them and carries them on its pinions. The Lord alone led him; no foreign god was with him. He made him ride on the heights of the land and fed him with the fruit of the fields. He nourished him with honey from the rock, and with oil from the flinty crag, with curds and milk from herd and flock and with fattened lambs and goats, with choice rams of Bashan and the finest kernels of wheat.

God reserves the best for us, so He asks that we reserve the best for Him in our sacrifice. The fact that Abel not only brought the firstborn, but he brought an animal that was fattened, demonstrated that he understood this principle; he took the time to prepare his sacrifice.

Romans 12:1:

I beseech you therefore, brethren, by the mercies of God, that you present your bodies a living sacrifice, holy, acceptable to God, which is your reasonable service.

We are to prepare for making our sacrifice to God; we should make the sacrifice to Him first, and then pay the bills on time. Plan on how you spend your money at the malls, so that you can bring an acceptable sacrifice to God. He has promised that if we put Him first, He will take care of everything else (Matthew 6:33) – and that includes the mortgage company and the car note.

#6 - Biblical Examples of Generous Givers[1]

1 Kings 17:7-16

And it happened after a while that the brook dried up, because there had been no rain in the land. Then the word of the LORD came to him, saying, "Arise, go to Zarephath, which belongs to Sidon, and dwell there. See, I have commanded a widow there to provide for you." So he arose and went to Zarephath. And when he came to the gate of the city, indeed a widow was there gathering sticks. And he called to her and said, "Please bring me a little water in a cup, that I may drink." And as she was going to get it, he called to her and said, "Please bring me a morsel of bread in your hand." So she said, "As the LORD your God lives, I do not have bread, only a handful of flour in a bin, and a little oil in a jar; and see, I am gathering a couple of sticks that I may go in and prepare it for myself and my son, that we may eat it, and die." And Elijah said to her, "Do not fear; go and do as you have said, but make me a small cake from it first, and bring it to me; and afterward make some for yourself and your son. For thus says the LORD God of Israel: "The bin of flour shall not be used up, nor shall the jar of oil run dry, until the day the LORD sends rain on the earth."' So she went away and did according to the word of Elijah; and she and he and her household ate for many days. The bin of flour was not used up, nor did the jar of oil run dry, according to the word of the LORD which He spoke by Elijah.

Ruth 2:5-9

Then Boaz said to his servant who was in charge of the reapers, "Whose young woman is this?" So the servant who was in charge of the reapers answered and said, "It is the young Moabite woman who came back with Naomi from the country of Moab. And she said, "Please let me glean and gather after the reapers among the sheaves." So she came and has continued from morning until now, though she rested a little in the house. Then Boaz said to Ruth, "You will listen, my daughter, will you not? Do not go to glean in another field, nor go from here, but stay close by my young women. Let your eyes be on the field which they reap, and go after them. Have I not commanded the young men not to touch you? And

when you are thirsty, go to the vessels and drink
from what the young men have drawn."

Mark 10:45

For even the Son of Man did not come to be served,
but to serve, and to give His life a ransom for many.

Mark 12:41-44

Now Jesus sat opposite the treasury and saw how
the people put money into the treasury. And many
who were rich put in much. Then one poor widow
came and threw in two mites, which make a quad-
rans. So He called His disciples to Himself and said
to them, "Assuredly, I say to you that this poor
widow has put in more than all those who have given
to the treasury; for they all put in out of their abun-
dance, but she out of her poverty put in all that she
had, her whole livelihood.

Acts 10:1-2

There was a certain man in Caesarea called
Cornelius, a centurion of what was called the Italian
Regiment, a devout man and one who feared God
with all his household, who gave alms generously to
the people, and prayed to God always.

2 Corinthians 8:1-6

Moreover, brethren, we make known to you the grace
of God bestowed on the churches of Macedonia: that

in a great trial of affliction the abundance of their joy and their deep poverty abounded in the riches of their liberality. For I bear witness that according to their ability, yes, and beyond their ability, they were freely willing, imploring us with much urgency that we would receive the gift and the fellowship of the ministering to the saints. And not only as we had hoped, but they first gave themselves to the Lord, and then to us by the will of God. So we urged Titus, that as he had begun, so he would also complete this grace in you as well.

Ephesians 5:1-2

Therefore be imitators of God as dear children. And walk in love, as Christ also has loved us and given Himself for us, an offering and a sacrifice to God for a sweet-smelling aroma.

Philippians 2:5-8

Let this mind be in you which was also in Christ Jesus, who, being in the form of God, did not consider it robbery to be equal with God, but made Himself of no reputation, taking the form of a bond-servant, and coming in the likeness of men. And being found in appearance as a man, He humbled Himself and became obedient to the point of death, even the death of the cross.

#7 – Thoughts on Riches[2]

THE WORLD'S VIEW OF RICHES	THE WORD'S VIEW OF RICHES
Money brings freedom.	The desire for money can be enslaving and lead to destruction; only Christ brings true freedom (John 8:36; 1 Tim. 6:7-10).
Money brings security.	Worldly wealth is very insecure; it quickly passes away (James 1:10). Real security is found in knowing and trusting God (Jer. 9:23,24; 1 Tim. 6:17-19).
Money is what matters.	Christ and the kingdom of God are what matters (Matt. 6:33; Phil. 3:7-10).
Money is power.	Power comes from being filled with the Holy Spirit (Acts 1:8; 3:1-10).
Money establishes not only your net worth, but also your worth as a person.	Your worth is based on what God says, not what your bank statement says (John 3:16; Eph. 1:3-14).
Money makes you successful.	Success comes from knowing and doing the will of God (Joshua 1:8).
Money gives you options.	God is the One who ultimately gives you options (Eph. 3:20).
Money brings happiness.	The happiness that money brings is short lived and does not lead to joy. And in the long term, money can actually produce "many sorrows" (1 Tim. 6:10). Lasting joy comes from knowing God (James 5:1-6; John 15:11; 16:24).
Money is your reward for your labors. Save it, and spend it on yourself.	Give as much as you can (Matt. 6:19-24; Acts 20:35; 2 Cor. 9:6-11; 1 Tim. 6:18).
Money is your possession. Spend it on whatever you want.	All that you have belongs to God, and He can do with it as He pleases. You are merely a steward of His possessions. (Ps. 24:1; Luke 19:11-27; 2 Cor. 5:10)

Final Thoughts

Throughout the pages of this book, I have outlined the Bible teachings on the spirituality of true stewardship as revealed to me by the Holy Spirit. Paul presented his case for Christ to the believers at Corinth, Ephesus, Colossus, and others — then in summation he used the term "therefore", which means but now. It signified that it was time for the believers to make a decision, based on the facts that he had presented. So, like Paul, I write: Therefore, my fellow believers — what do you do then? Do you continue to withhold your best from God? Do you allow the Holy Spirit to lead you to give your best to God? Remember, your eligibility for eternal life is based on your adherence to God's principles of stewardship.

And to the leaders of God's people, keep His principles of stewardship pure and spiritual; do not allow the father of all lies, the devil, to deceive you into choosing the world's counterfeits of fundraising and philanthropy. The Bible does not sanction them as alternatives to God's ordained principles of stewardship.

References:

1. *The Bible and Money* - http://www.generousgiving.org
2. *The Nelson Study Bible, NKJV* - Bible commentaries.

Appendix

Here is some additional material to assist stewardship leaders with the planning and organization of the stewardship program for their organization.

Stewardship Survey for Members - Sample

Part 1 - Tasks of the Church

1: Disagree, 2: Some what Disagree, 3: Some what Agree 4: Agree

	1	2	3	4
1. _____(your church name here) is a warm and caring church, and demonstrates that by acts of charity and service for persons in need.	1	2	3	4
2. My church is meeting the spiritual and physical needs of our community.	1	2	3	4
3. I would be better educated about the needs of my church after a stewardship seminar.	1	2	3	4
4. The appeals from the pulpit and the sermons on stewardship have challenged me to re-assess my giving.	1	2	3	4
5. My church assists the members in discovering their gifts and talents.	1	2	3	4
6. My church encourages the members to understand the need to use their time, talents/gifts and financial resources in Christian stewardship.	1	2	3	4

Part 2 - You and Your Stewardship Experience as a Christian

7. Do you know what your spiritual gift(s) or talent(s) are?

☐ Yes ☐ No

8. If yes to #7, please select the item(s) that best describes your spiritual gift(s) or talent(s) that you believe God has blessed you with:

☐ Teaching ☐ Counseling / Motivating others

☐ Finances ☐ Influence

☐ Prayer ☐ Preaching

☐ Prophecy ☐ Singing

☐ Comforting ☐ Other

If Other, please specify:

_____

_____

_____

9. If yes to #7, are you using your spiritual gifts for God's glory and the building up of Christ's Church?

☐ once in a while ☐ frequently ☐ as much as I can

10. Do you thank God for His provision and blessing in your life?

☐ never ☐ sometimes ☐ often ☐ regularly

11. Why do you desire God's blessing in your life?

☐ so I wouldn't have problems ☐ so I can be happy

☐ so I can be a blessing to others

12. How much time a week to you devote to God (Bible reading, prayer, private worship) and to His service (corporate worship or service to God in or out of the church)?

☐ less than 2 hrs ☐ 2 to 4 hrs ☐ 4 to 6 hrs ☐ more than 6 hrs

13. How much of your income do you give back to God out of love and gratitude?

☐ less than 5% ☐ between 5 and 10% ☐ 10% ☐ more than 10%

14. Compared to what you spend on recreation (vacations, hobbies, sports, entertainment), how much do you give to God and His work?

☐ less ☐ equal amount ☐ more ☐ much more

15. How do you see _____ 's (your church name here) Stewardship
    Committee:

Please select one:

☐ As a committee that works to create better stewardship knowledge for the church, and to help the members to achieve spiritual fulfillment through the practice of stewardship,

OR

☐ As a committee that functions as a fundraising committee, which is willing to plan and implement fundraising opportunities for the church.

16. How long have you attended _____ (Your Church name here)?

☐ 0-3 yrs   ☐ 4-7 yrs   ☐ 8-10 yrs   ☐ 10+ yrs

17. Are you a member of this church?

☐ Yes   ☐ No

18. Would you be willing to attend a stewardship seminar at this church?

☐ Yes   ☐ No

YOUR COMMENTS

<u>Please comment</u> below on issues (if any) that you feel <u>were not addressed</u> in this survey:

_____

_____

_____

_____

_____

_____

_____

_____

_____

Thank You Letter for Every Contributing Church Member

Dear Mr. and Mrs. John Doe and Family,

I wish to commend you for demonstrating your adherence to the principles of stewardship. Because of your faithfulness at *The Church Of Faithful stewards*, we believe that God is blessing you and your family as He promised in Proverbs 1:33.

With God's help and your regular support throughout the year, we have been able to bless others through our church's ministries as well as fulfill our financial obligations.

In addition, our church has been able to:
- Achievement 1
- Achievement 2
- Achievement 3

Again, We thank you for your commitment and support and pray that the Lord will enrich your spiritual experience as you continue to adhere to His principles of true stewardship.

God loves a cheerful giver — 2 Corinthians 9:7.

Sincerely,

John D. Motivator,   **Jane D. Encourager,**
Pastor   **Stewardship Director**

Church Of Faithful stewards

Stewardship Is God's Way of Guaranteeing Financial Freedom for Us

The list below should be printed on one page (letter size), high quality, non-glossy paper and given to each member or family; advise them to frame it or put it on their refrigerator, any place where they can see it regularly.

Top 10 List of Things You Can Do to Gain Financial Freedom in YYYY. (Example 2003)

10. Build a budget— Develop a monthly budget and make it your guide to financial freedom. *Commit your works to the LORD, and your thoughts will be established* (Proverbs 16:3).

Whatever you think your financial goals may be, you will not successfully achieve them without first understanding God's financial principles found in the Bible. When you do understand them, develop lifestyle goals that reflect them and work out a written plan to do so (a budget). He will lead you to financial freedom.

9. Reduce your use—don't use your credit card so much. Develop discipline in your spending habits. Commit to go no further in debt, and you will begin to reverse the process that produced your debt. *The rich rules over the poor, and the borrower is servant to the lender* (Proverbs 22:7).

Remember that the problem is not credit cards but the misuse of credit cards.

8. Get a grip—Spending (especially for indulgences) doesn't lift depression. In fact, after the initial rush, it can make things worse. *He who loves pleasure will be a poor man; He who loves wine and oil will not be rich* (Proverbs 21:17).

7. Look at your paycheck—Write the bottom-line number down, and then spend less than that. *I spoke to you in your prosperity, but you said, "I will not hear." This has been your manner from your youth, that you did not obey My voice* (Jeremiah 22:21).

Don't spend more than you make, don't borrow, and you'll be on the road to financial freedom.

6. Cook a meal—Discover the kitchen occasionally and reduce the number of restaurant visits. *Poverty and shame will come to him who disdains correction, but he who regards a rebuke will be honored* (Proverbs 13:18).

5. Get in the car—Take a local vacation this year. *A man's heart plans his way, but the LORD directs his step* (Proverbs 16:9).

People spend hundreds of dollars they can't afford to travel thousands of miles to see things they might not remember next year.

4. Don't keep up with the Jones's—They're in debt, too (and you can be sure they won't make your payments for you)! *Again, I saw that for all toil and every skillful work a man is envied by his neighbor. This also is vanity and grasping for the wind* (Ecclesiastes 4:4).

Envy is the desire to achieve based on the observation of other people's successes. Don't set your goals based on what others have. In the long run, envy and covetousness will still leave you empty because you'll never have enough.

3. Keep the "ultimate driving machine"—You know…the one that's paid for. Most people buy new cars because they don't budget car-maintenance money for the car they own; when it breaks down they can't afford to repair it. You may say, "But it's zero money down!" But remember, those new car little- or no-money-down financial gimmicks require some budget-destroying payments. *For which of you, intending to build a tower, does not sit down first and count the cost, whether he has enough to finish it?* (Luke 14:28).

2. Pray each day before you pay—Emotional and spiritual balance will lead to financial freedom. So ask God to guide you and give you strength to follow the first eight (8) steps. *In everything give thanks; for this is the will of God in Christ Jesus for you* (1 Thessalonians 5:18).

And the Number One Thing You Can Do to Find Financial Freedom in YYYY (Example 2003):

1. Give it back —Set your priorities straight; first, set aside the tithe and your free will offering. Give to God's work; it's His money anyway.

Loosen up those purse strings; it will help loosen the grip money might have on your heart. *Let them do good, that they be rich in good works, ready to give, willing to share* (1 Timothy 6:18).

Don't give in order to get. However, you'll find that when you do give, God will provide you with more to give. *My little children, let us not love in word or in tongue, but in deed and in truth* (1 John 3:18).

References:

1. *Christian Stewardship of Possessions – Compelled by the Love of Christ* by David J. Valleskey (August 1989).